T0365297

Cambridge Elements

Elements in Applied Evolutionary Science
edited by
David F. Bjorklund
Florida Atlantic University

EVOLUTION AND THE FATE OF HUMANKIND

Peter A. Corning
Institute for the Study of Complex Systems

THE EVOLUTION INSTITUTE

CAMBRIDGE
UNIVERSITY PRESS

CAMBRIDGE
UNIVERSITY PRESS

Shaftesbury Road, Cambridge CB2 8EA, United Kingdom

One Liberty Plaza, 20th Floor, New York, NY 10006, USA

477 Williamstown Road, Port Melbourne, VIC 3207, Australia

314–321, 3rd Floor, Plot 3, Splendor Forum, Jasola District Centre,
New Delhi – 110025, India

103 Penang Road, #05–06/07, Visioncrest Commercial, Singapore 238467

Cambridge University Press is part of Cambridge University Press & Assessment,
a department of the University of Cambridge.

We share the University's mission to contribute to society through the pursuit
of education, learning and research at the highest international levels of excellence.

www.cambridge.org
Information on this title: www.cambridge.org/9781009613842

DOI: 10.1017/9781009613835

First published 2025

A catalogue record for this publication is available from the British Library

ISBN 978-1-009-61384-2 Hardback
ISBN 978-1-009-61381-1 Paperback
ISSN 2752-9428 (online)
ISSN 2752-941X (print)

Cambridge University Press & Assessment has no responsibility for the persistence
or accuracy of URLs for external or third-party internet websites referred to in this
publication and does not guarantee that any content on such websites is, or will
remain, accurate or appropriate.

Evolution and the Fate of Humankind

Elements in Applied Evolutionary Science

DOI: 10.1017/9781009613835
First published online: February 2025

Peter A. Corning
Institute for the Study of Complex Systems

Author for correspondence: Peter A. Corning, pacorning@complexsystems.org

Abstract: In recent years we have come to understand better the forces that have shaped biological evolution over the course of time. Evolved purposiveness (teleonomy) in living systems themselves has been an important influence. Cooperative effects (synergies) of various kinds have also been influential. And the bioeconomics (functional costs and benefits) have been important constraints. Now we are facing a mounting survival crisis that may determine the future of life on Earth. We need to make a major course change, utilizing our insights into these important influences. Here is a review, and a "prescription."

Keywords: evolution, teleonomy, synergy, bioeconomics, climate change

ISBNs: 9781009613842 (HB), 9781009613811 (PB), 9781009613835 (OC)
ISSNs: 2752-9428 (online), 2752-941X (print)

Contents

Introduction

When astronomers and astrophysicists realized that there were large unexplained anomalies in the universe, they invented an unobserved dark matter and dark energy to explain them. They still haven't observed dark matter and dark energy but are convinced that they must exist. Or could their theories about the universe be wrong?

For evolutionary biologists, random genetic mutations came to occupy a similar place in explaining biological evolution during the era of the so-called "Modern Synthesis" during the twentieth century. However, we now know that random genetic changes have had little influence in evolution. There are many far more important factors, including the actions of living systems themselves as purposeful "agents" and the many kinds of cooperative effects (synergies) in living systems.

In this volume I will draw upon our updated understanding of evolution to address our growing climate crisis and to "prescribe" a potential strategy for responding to it.

I should note that the term "agency" was imported into biology from the social sciences and philosophy, and it is entangled with theories of "mind," human cognition, intentional behavior, rationality, rational choice theory, and artificial intelligence, among other things. However, there have been some useful efforts to sort all this out for biologists. Walsh (2015), for instance, stresses that agency in biology refers to the goal-directed behavior of living organisms – their ability to pursue goals and to respond appropriately to conditions in their environments. Agency is fundamentally an "ecological phenomenon," he says, and he identifies three key properties of biological agency: (1) goals, (2) "affordances" which are determined by both the organism and its environment and (3) the organism's "repertoire" of behavioral responses. Okasha (2018), likewise, identifies three rationales for applying the term "agency" in biology: (1) goal-directed activities in organisms with a "unified" goal, (2) behavioral flexibility, and (3) traits that are adaptations serving intermediate "sub-purposes" related to the overarching goal. (For more on "agency," see the footnote.[1])

---

[1] I would add to this the following points: Because life is a contingent phenomenon, living organisms must actively pursue opportunities (resources) in their environments and must be able to avoid, or cope with challenges and threats of various kinds. Agency is thus an evolved capability that enables a living system to respond to the variability and changing conditions in relation to needed resources and challenges/threats in its environment. (Mobility in an organism also greatly increases this challenge, needless to say.) Agency in living systems requires: (1) the detection or "perception" of variations in internal and external conditions; (2) the ability to discriminate among these perceptions ("information"); (3) the ability to purposefully vary behavior, or actions; and (4) "control" – or the ability to link information with actions (cf., the

1 "Life Ascending"

Here I will begin with what is known about the origins of life, consider the vexed question of Vitalism in evolution, explore the role of teleonomy (evolved purposiveness) in evolution, review the evidence for the role of various kinds of cooperative effects (synergies) in evolution, consider the costs and benefits (the bioeconomics) of evolution, revisit Darwin's often misunderstood theories about evolution, reconsider the rise of humankind, and end with a prescription for our growing environmental crisis, with particular reference to Benjamin Franklin's famous warning before the American Revolution: "Unite or Die."

In his two important books on the subject, biochemist Nick Lane (2009, 2015), discussed at length the evidence for how life arose. As he put it: "Life itself transformed our planet from the battered and fiery rock that once orbited a young star ... Life itself turned our planet blue and green, as tiny photosynthetic bacteria cleansed the oceans of air and sea and filled them with oxygen. Powered by this new source of energy, life erupted" (Lane, 2009: 1).

How life first arose has long been debated, of course. In the modern era, the debate began, perhaps, with the Nobel physicist Erwin Schrödinger's wartime lectures and famous 1944 book, *What Is Life?* Schrödinger pioneered the idea that ordered energy (now called negative entropy, or "negentropy") was an essential factor. Life is, among other things, a thermodynamic process. Today, we commonly refer to it as "metabolism." Many years later, biologists Humberto Maturana and Francisco Varela (1980/1973) identified another important property of living systems. They called it "autopoiesis" or self-making. Life has a form of autonomy, they proposed. Today the term "agency" is commonplace.

A more elaborate effort to explain the rise of living systems was provided by the little-known Hungarian theoretical biologist Tibor Gánti (1971). His three-part "Chemoton" model included an autocatalytic network for metabolism, machinery for controlling growth and self-replication, and a protective envelope to shield the system from the environment. In other words, he proposed a cooperative (synergistic) system. Some theorists, notably including John

---

cybernetic model of goal-oriented, "feedback" driven behavior). Agency is not dependent upon having a "brain." It can be based upon simple decision rules. However, its effectiveness can be greatly enhanced by being able to draw upon prior learning and memory, along with in situ cognitive and problem-solving skills. Agency will be favored by natural selection in relation to the degree of variability and novelty in the opportunities and threats in any given environmental context. But it is also a costly trait. It requires energy and functionally specialized biomass that must be built and maintained over time. Therefore, it will atrophy, or will not evolve at all, in conditions where it is not clearly advantageous for survival and reproduction. Illustrations of these points can be found in such diverse living entities as macrophages, bacteria at hydrothermal vents, slime molds, sea floor sponges, land plants, insects, fish, birds, and mammals.

Maynard Smith and Eörs Szathmáry (1999), argue that an additional require-ment for life is the ability to evolve, when there is variation that can be differentially selected. I would add that life must also be able to respond to "feedback" and to changes in the environment. It must be sentient.

Two of the major alternative theories about the origin of life depend on yet another synergistic effect, an external catalyst. One is the "surface metabolism" theory of Günter Wächtershäuser (1988). He proposed that ancient Earth, with high concentrations of metallic compounds, may have provided important catalysts. The subsequent discovery of hydrothermal vents on the ocean floor lent credence to this idea. The other theory, proposed by geochemist Mike Russell (2006) and his colleagues (Martin & Russell, 2003; Koonin & Martin, 2005), involves a different kind of "metabolism first" theory, namely, deep-sea alkaline vents and the CO_2 in the ancient oceans. In effect, this provided an abundant source of free energy. It is a compelling idea. Most recently, biochem-ist Addy Pross (2024) has suggested that consciousness in evolution may have a biochemical basis.

These and other theories advanced in recent years, like the proposal that life was "seeded" by compounds brought from outer space by the once abundant meteors (see Powner, Gerland & Sutherland, 2009), make it seem even more likely that a synergistic combination of elements for the catalyzing life arose together in the early environment.

The Evolution of Prokaryotes

The evolution of prokaryotes (bacteria and their cousins, archaea) perhaps 3.7 billion years ago (some theorists say even earlier) was another major step in biological evolution. The prokaryotes were the first complete organisms, and they are still with us today. Indeed, they are the most productive form of life on Earth, with an estimated total biomass that outweighs all other fauna and flora combined (see Corning, 2018). Prokaryotes are also highly creative and adaptable. They invented many important biotechnologies, including photosynthesis, nitrogen fixing, fermentation, and cellular damage repair, and they can synthesize many different kinds of minerals. More important for our purpose, they invented various forms of collective action, from the division of labor to pack-hunting behaviors. It was the primordial "collective survival enterprise" (Corning, 2018: 102–104). As Baluška, Miller, and Reber (2023a, 2023b) have stressed in detail, sentience and cognitive abilities can be found in all living organisms. Some theorists even see evolution as a cognition-based process (e.g., Miller, 2023).

The next major transition in evolution was the emergence, some 1.8–2.0 bil-lion years ago, of eukaryotes – complex single-celled organisms with an array of specialized internal organelles and with genes in a sequestered nucleus. But the most important innovation was the role played by their symbiotic partners, the mitochondria, which provide the eukaryotes with an abundant source of energy. This enabled them to grow vastly larger than the prokaryotes – an important synergy of scale – and to become specialists in even larger multicellular organisms, another transition in biological size and complexity. "Symbiogenesis" represented an important cooperative partnership (Margulis, 1970, 1981, 1998; Margulis & Fester, 1991; Margulis & Sagan, 1995, 2002). (See the footnote.[2])

The emergence of multicellular organisms was another synergistic innovation. Among the innumerable examples, consider the human body. It involves an extraordinary combination of labor by an estimated 30 trillion cells of some 210 different kinds that are organized into an extraordinarily complex system of functionally differentiated parts, including 10 different specialized organ systems (Corning, 2018: 112–113). A human being, or any other multicellular organism (from earthworms to elephants), is fundamentally a cooperative effect, a synergistic system.

Finally, the synergies were raised to a new level with the emergence of behavioral cooperation and social organization among individuals of the same species – including everything from pack hunting to joint nesting, collective migration, collective defense against predators, and much more. One well-known example is the so-called leaf-cutter ants (pictured on the cover of my 2018 book, *Synergistic Selection: How Cooperation Has Shaped Evolution and the Rise of Humankind*). Another example is the recent discovery of underground cooperative systems among forest trees (see especially Shilthuizen, 2018).

2 Designers versus Tinkerers in Evolution

"Vitalism" is the doctrine that proceeds from the premise that living organisms are fundamentally different from nonliving entities because they contain some nonphysical element or are governed by different principles than inanimate things. Frequently used are such terms as *élan vital* (coined by Vitalist Henri Bergson) or a "vital spark." Among other things, this doctrine has come to be associated with the Intelligent Design movement, as well as various therapeutic medical treatments. Since the mid-twentieth century, though, Vitalism has been considered a pseudoscience. Evolution can be characterized as a process of

---

[2] Although the basic idea of symbiogenesis, and even the term itself, traces back to a school of nineteenth- and early twentieth-century Russian botanists, including A.S. Famintsyn (1907a, 1907b, 1918), Konstantin Mereschkovsky (1909, 1920), and B.M. Kozo-Polyansky (1924, 1932), their pioneering work was generally not known to Western scientists until recent decades.

biological "tinkering" (or trial-and-error) over eons of time, in Nobel biologist François Jacob's (1977) classic term.

Now it seems that Vitalism is being revitalized. Daniel Witt (2024), a persistent advocate for the idea of Intelligent Design, has suggested that recent publications on purposiveness (teleonomy) in living systems show that Vitalism is "making a comeback." Witt does not seem to believe that teleonomy in living systems could be an evolved biological trait – a product of natural selection. Perhaps he did not read my extensive introductory/overview chapter: "Teleonomy in Evolution: "The Ghost in the Machine" in P. A. Corning et al., eds. *Evolution "On Purpose": Teleonomy in Living Systems.* (Cambridge, MA. The MIT Press, 2023). As the eminent twentieth-century biologist Theodosius Dobzhansky long ago explained:

> Purposefulness, or teleology, does not exist in nonliving nature. It is universal in the living world. It would make no sense to talk of the purposiveness or adaptation of stars, mountains, or the laws of physics. Adaptedness of living beings is too obvious to be overlooked . . .. Living beings have an *internal*, or natural, teleology. Organisms, from the smallest bacterium to man, arise from similar organisms by ordered growth and development. Their internal teleology has accumulated in the history of their lineage. On the assumption that all existing life is derived from one primordial ancestor, the internal teleology of an organism is the outcome of approximately three and a half billion years of organic evolution . . .. Internal teleology is not a static property of life. Its advances and recessions can be observed, sometimes induced experimentally, and analyzed scientifically like other biological phenomena. (Dobzhansky, 1977: 95–96)

In sum, purposiveness (or teleonomy) in living systems is a product of evolution and natural selection. It has nothing to do with any purported external Vitalism.

3 Teleonomy in Evolution

The Ghost in the Machine is the title of a provocative book by the polymath and famed twentieth-century novelist Arthur Koestler (1967), in which he disputed the then-fashionable view, often attributed to Descartes, that the human mind is a dualistic, non-material entity. (Koestler's ironic title was borrowed from the philosopher Gilbert Ryle.) Koestler argued that, on the contrary, the mind is embedded in and is a product of the natural world.

This distinctive title underscores the cardinal fact that teleonomy (or evolved purposiveness) in biological evolution is not simply a product of natural selection. It is also an important cause of natural selection and has been a major shaping influence in evolution over time. Natural selection is not an exogenous force or "mechanism." It is an outcome of the relationships and interactions between purposeful living organisms – agents if you will – and their lived-in environments, inclusive of other organisms.

The term "teleonomy" was originally coined by the biologist Colin Pittendrigh in connection with the landmark 1957 conference on behavior in evolution (Roe & Simpson, eds., 1958). Pittendrigh was seeking to draw a contrast between an "external" teleology (Aristotelian or religious) and the "internal" purposiveness and goal-directedness of living systems, which are products of the evolutionary process and of natural selection.

Many theorists over the years have expressed supportive views, as Samir Okasha (2018) has documented in his book-length study, *Agents and Goals in Evolution* (see also Walsh, 2015). For instance, the Nobel biologist Jacques Monod (1971: 9) concluded that "one of the most fundamental characteristics common to all living things [is] that of being endowed with a project, or a purpose." Likewise, the biologist Ernst Mayr, one of the founding fathers of the so-called Modern Synthesis in evolutionary biology, wrote, "goal directed behaviour ... is extremely widespread in the natural world; most activity connected with migration, food-getting, courtship, ontogeny, and all phases of reproduction is characterized by such goal orientation" (Mayr, 1988: 45; see also Mayr, 1963).

Over the years, many theorists have interpreted teleonomy broadly. Pittendrigh (1958) himself characterized it as a "fundamental property" and defining feature of all biological phenomena, including behavior. Similarly, Monod, in his influential book, *Chance and Necessity*, concluded: "All the structures, all the performances, all the activities contributing to the essential project [of life] will hence be called 'teleonomic' .... It is the very definition of living beings" (Monod, 1971: 9,14). As an example, he pointed to the central nervous system.

However, Mayr (1974), in his classic essay on "Teleological and Teleonomic: A New Analysis," opposed such a broad definition. Mayr framed teleonomy as requiring a preexisting goal and "something material" that guides and controls a "process" to a "determinable end." In living organisms, he said, this a priori goal entails a "program" – an analogy Mayr borrowed from computers. It is the teleonomic program that is responsible for directing the process of developing a phenotype and its behavior, although an "open program" (as Mayr called it) allows for the influence of learning and experience (and other "disturbances"). To illustrate his definition, Mayr alluded to the science of cybernetics, or goal-directed control systems. He also insisted that a teleonomic program – an obvious euphemism for the genome – could only have a one-way flow of information, and that developmental influences are highly restricted. "The inheritance of acquired characters becomes quite unthinkable." (In fact, we now know this is not true.)

Mayr was adamant that it was inappropriate to attribute purposiveness to the process of evolution itself, or to the influence of natural selection, and he opposed applying the term teleonomy to any "static" biological system (presumably meaning the structural components of an organism). He cited the central nervous system as a contrary example. Thus, he implicitly contradicted Monod. Mayr also insisted that "It is misleading and quite inadmissible to designate such broadly generalized concepts as survival or reproductive success as definite and specified goals. Teleonomy does not exist outside the ultimately determinative influence of DNA and the genetic 'program'."

In other words, Mayr was supportive of the gene centered, one-way, bottom-up evolutionary paradigm, commonly referred to as the Modern Synthesis, or Neo-Darwinism, which predominated at the time in evolutionary theory, and he seemed to exclude what he called "proximate" causes from exerting a direct influence on "ultimate" causes (natural selection and evolution). Indeed, in an earlier paper, Mayr (1961) had identified only two categories of legitimate "evolutionary causes" – "genetic causes" and "ecological causes." Mayr's adherence to what the Nobel biologist Francis Crick (1970) termed the "central dogma" of evolutionary theory and his radical separation of proximate and ultimate causation is, in fact, no longer tenable, (as detailed in Laland et al., 2011, 2013; also, Calcott, 2013a, 2013b; Corning 2019, 2020).

4 Some Ghosts in the Machine

Among other things, there is growing evidence, championed especially by biologist Lynn Margulis (1970, 1993, 1998; Margulis & Fester, 1991), that symbiosis – cooperative relationships between organisms of different species with complementary capabilities – is a widespread phenomenon in the natural world, and that "symbiogenesis" has played a major causal role in shaping the evolutionary trajectory over time (see also Sapp, 1994, 2009; Margulis & Sagan, 1995, 2002; Gontier, 2007; Carrapiço, 2010; Archibald, 2014). Symbiogenesis theory shifts the locus of innovation away from "random" changes in genes, genomes, and the "classical" model of natural selection to the "purposeful" behavioral actions of the phenotypes and their functional consequences.

An even greater challenge to Neo-Darwinism and the Modern Synthesis arose with the discovery that single celled prokaryotes are profligate sharers of genetic material via "horizontal" (or lateral) gene transmission and do not strictly follow the pattern of competition and Mendelian ("vertical") inheritance from parent to offspring, as the Modern Synthesis assumes (Sapp, 2009; Koonin, 2011; Crisp et al., 2015). As the biologist Eugene Koonin (2009) concluded, all the central tenets of the Modern Synthesis break down with prokaryotes and the findings of comparative genomics. The prokaryote world can best be described as a single, vast, interconnected gene pool, he argues.

The rise of evolutionary developmental biology (evo-devo for short) has also produced serious challenges to the Modern Synthesis, including the discovery that there are many deep homologies and highly conserved structural gene complexes in the genome (some of which are universal in living systems), and especially the extensive work on morphological development and "phenotypic plasticity" (Müller & Newman, 2003; West Eberhard, 2003; 2005a, 2005b; Koonin, 2011; Bateson & Gluckman, 2011). There is also the burgeoning evidence that the genome is in fact a "two-way read-write system," as the biologist James Shapiro (2011, 2013) characterizes it. The extensive and rapidly increasing evidence of epigenetic inheritance (changes in the phenotype that are transmitted to the germ plasm in the next generation) also falsifies the one-way, gene-centered theory (see Jablonka & Raz, 2009; Jablonka, 2013; Noble, 2013, 2015, 2017, 2018; Jablonka & Lamb, 2014; Walsh, 2015; Huneman & Walsh, 2017).

Recent progress in microbiology has also shown that an overwhelming majority of DNA changes in the genome are the result of internal regulatory and control networks, not random mutations and incremental, "additive" selection. In fact, rapid genome alteration and restructuring can be achieved by a variety of mobile DNA "modules" – transposons (McClintock & Moore, 1987), integrons, CRISPRS, retroposons, variable antigen determinants, and more (Craig, 2002; Sapp, 2009; Craig et al., 2015; Shapiro, 2011, 2013; Koonin, 2011, 2016; Noble, 2017). It is now also apparent that individual cells have a great variety of internal regulatory and control capabilities that can significantly influence cell development and the phenotype. They may even provide feedback that modifies the genome and affects subsequent generations (Shapiro, 1991, 2011; Noble, 2006, 2011, 2017, 2018; Pan & Zhang, 2009; Gladyshev & Arkhipova, 2011; Koonin, 2011). Particularly significant are the discoveries related to the influence of exosomes, which resemble Darwin's speculative ideas of pangenesis and the role of internal migratory "gemmules" in reproduction (Edelstein et al., eds. 1999). Exosomes also clearly violate the so-called Weismann Barrier (1892), the assumption that genetic change can only be a one-way process.

As Shapiro (2011: 2) emphasizes, "The capacity of living organisms to alter their own heredity is undeniable. Our current ideas about evolution have to incorporate this basic fact of life." Shapiro cites some thirty-two different examples of what he refers to as "natural genetic engineering," including immune system responses, chromosomal rearrangements, diversity generating retroelements, the actions of transposons, genome restructuring, whole genome duplication, and symbiotic DNA integration (see also Shapiro, 2013). Likewise, Jablonka and Lamb (2014) identify four distinct "Lamarckian" modes of inheritance: (1) directed adaptive mutations, (2) the inheritance of characters acquired during development and the lifetime of the individual, (3) behavioral inheritance through social learning, and (4) language-based information transmission. All this prompted biologist Kevin Laland and his colleagues to publish two major critiques of Mayr's proximate-ultimate dichotomy (Laland et al., 2011, 2013). These critics argue that proximate and ultimate causes are interpenetrated and that the one-way causal model associated with the Modern Synthesis and Neo-Darwinism should be replaced with one that recognizes a major role for "reciprocal causation" (see also Calcott, 2013a, 2013b).

5 Teleonomy and Natural Selection

To fully appreciate the causal role of teleonomic influences in evolution, I believe it would be helpful to revisit the concept of natural selection. The neo-Darwinian definition of the term has always tended to be narrow, gene-centered, and circular. Evolution is defined as "a change in gene frequencies" in a given "deme," or breeding population, and natural selection is defined as a "mechanism" which produces changes in gene frequencies. As the biologist John H. Campbell put it in a review: "Changes in the frequencies of alleles by natural selection *are* evolution" (Campbell 1994: 86). By implication, it followed that mutations and related molecular-level changes – subject to the "approval" of natural selection – are the only important sources of novelty in evolution. Natural selection is in turn represented as being an external "mechanism," or "force" out there in the environment somewhere.

The dominant theme in this paradigm is a competitive "struggle for existence," as Darwin characterized it. (The associated catch phrase, "survival of the fittest," was actually coined by a contemporary theorist, Herbert Spencer, but it was also used by Darwin in later editions of his masterwork). Indeed, the term "Darwinian" is often treated as a synonym for any competitive, winner-take-all dynamic. However, it happens that this is only one of Darwin's two distinct evolutionary theories. The other theory, less appreciated, actually originated with his prominent predecessor, Lamarck (see also discussion further).

However, natural selection is not a mechanism; it is a happening. It does not *do* anything; nothing is ever actively selected (although sexual selection and artificial selection are special cases). Nor can the sources of causation be localized either within an organism or externally in the environment. In fact, the term "natural selection," as Darwin used it, is a metaphor – an "umbrella term" that identifies a fundamental aspect of the evolutionary process. The ground zero premise of evolutionary biology is that life is, in essence, a contingent "survival enterprise." Living organisms are inherently contingent dynamic phenomena that must actively seek to survive and reproduce. This existential problem requires that they must be goal-directed in an immediate, proximate sense. Thus, natural selection refers to whatever functionally signifi- cant factors are responsible in a given context for causing differential survival and reproduction. The well-known Behaviorist psychologist B.F. Skinner (1981) called it "selection by consequences." Properly conceptualized, these causal "factors" are intensely interactional and relational; they are defined by both the organism(s) and their environment(s).

A Classic Illustration

A classic and still-relevant textbook illustration involves the so-called "peppered moth." Until the Industrial Revolution, a "cryptic" (light- colored) species of the peppered moth (*Biston betularia*) predominated in the English countryside over a darker "melanic" form (*Biston carbonaria*). The mottled wing coloration of *B. betularia* provided camouflage from avian predators as the moths rested on the trunks of lichen-encrusted trees. The darker, melanic form obviously did not share this advantage. But as industrial soot progressively blackened the tree trunks in areas close to expanding industrial cities, the relative frequency of the two forms was reversed; the birds began to prey more heavily on the now more visible peppered moths (Kettlewell 1955, 1973).

The question is, where in this example was natural selection "located"? The short answer is that natural selection encompasses the entire *configuration* of factors that combined to influence differential survival and reproduction. In this case, an alteration in the relationship between the coloration of the trees and the wing pigmentation of the moths, as a consequence of industrial pollution, was an important proximate factor. But this factor was important only because of the inflexible resting behavior of the moths and the feeding habits and perceptual abilities of the birds. Had the moths been subject only to insect-eating bats that use "sonar" to catch insects on the wing, rather than a visual detection system, the change in background coloration would not have been significant. Nor would it have been significant were there not genetically based patterns of wing coloration in the two forms that were available for "selection." (It should also be noted that a subsequent challenge to Kettlewell's methods and the validity of his findings was resolved when a British geneticist, Mike Majerus, undertook a study that confirmed the original results.) See Chris Hurley and Stephen Montgomery (2009), "Peppered Moths & Melanism."[3]

Accordingly, the ongoing survival challenge (again, Darwin referred to it as "the struggle for existence") imposes a potential constraint on all aspects of the process of living. Every feature, or trait, of a given organism can be viewed in terms of its relationship (for better or worse, or not at all) to this fundamental, built-in, inescapable problem. Accordingly, natural selection differentially favors proximate functional "means" over time that serve the ultimate biological "end" of survival and reproduction. Indeed, the very term "adaptation" is commonly defined as a feature that advances some process or deals with some challenge related to survival and reproduction.

The Neo-Darwinian definition also tends to equate natural selection and evolution with genetic changes, rather than viewing evolution more expansively as a multileveled process in which genes, other molecular factors, genomes, developmental ("epigenetic") influences, mature phenotypes, and the natural environment interact with one another and evolve together in a dynamic relationship of mutual and reciprocal causation, including (in the current jargon) "upward" causation, "downward" causation, and even "horizontal" causation (for example, in predator–prey interactions or between symbionts). (See especially Vane-Wright 1996, 2009.) The rise of "multi-level selection theory" in biology during the past three decades has served as a helpful corrective to classic Neo-Darwinism (see especially D.S. Wilson, 1997; also, Okasha, 2006; Traulsen & Nowak, 2006). So, also is the extensive work on "niche construction theory" (Odling-Smee et al., 1996, 2003; Laland et al., 1999), as well as the growing literature on the role of cultural influences in evolution, culminating in humankind (Kingdon, 1993; Boyd & Richerson, 2005, 2009; Corning, 2005, 2014, 2018; Richerson & Boyd, 2005; Boyd et al., 2011; Laland et al., 2010; Henrich, 2016; Laland, 2017).

Another way of framing it is that evolution involves four distinct categories of functional variation (1) molecular-genetic variation, (2) phenotypic variation (inclusive of developmental, physiological, and behavioral/cultural variations), (3) ecological (environmental) variations, and (4) differential survival and reproduction as an outcome of the specific organism–environment relationships and interactions in a given context. Furthermore, the causal arrows between these domains can go in both directions.

Thus, many things, at many different levels, may be responsible for bringing about changes in an organism–environment relationship, and differential

---

[3] www.christs.cam.ac.uk/darwin200/pages/index.php?page_id=g5 I thank Prof. Dick Vane-Wright for this information.

survival. It could be a functionally significant mutation, a chromosomal trans-position, a change in the physical environment that affects development, a change in one species that affects another species, or it could be a change in behavior that results in a new organism–environment relationship. In fact, a whole sequence of changes may ripple through a pattern of relationships. For instance, a climate change might alter the ecology, which might prompt a behavioral shift to a new habitat, which might encourage an alteration in nutritional habits, which might precipitate changes in the interactions among different species, resulting ultimately in the differential survival and reproduc-tion of organisms with differing morphological characters and the genes that support them.

"Darwin's Finches"

An in vivo illustration of this causal dynamic can be found in the long-running research program in the Galápagos Islands among "Darwin's finches" (Weiner, 1994). It is well known that birds often use their beaks as tools, and that their beaks tend to be specialized for whatever food sources are available in a given environment. In the Galápagos Islands, the zoologist Peter Grant and his wife and colleague have observed many changes over the years among its fourteen closely related finch species in response to environmental changes (Grant & Grant, 1979, 1989, 1993, 2002). During drought periods, for instance, small seeds become scarce, and the most abundant food source consists of much larger, tougher seeds that must be cracked open to get at their kernels. Birds with larger, stronger beaks have a functional advantage, and this is the proximate cause of their differential survival during a drought.

In sum, natural selection is focused on the functional causes of differential survival and reproduction (the bioeconomics), and it is agnostic about how and why this has occurred in any given context. Contrary to Mayr, the survival imperative can indeed be posited as an overarching goal in living systems (without any scare quotes or "as ifs"), inclusive of the proximate teleonomic phenomena that are, in fact, causal influences in natural selection. The basic unit of analysis in this alternative paradigm is not the genes but interdependent living "systems" and their parts – along with their external "affordances" and depend-encies (Rosen, 1970, 1991; Bateson, 2004, 2005; Corning, 2005, 2018; Noble, 2006, 2012, 2017; Capra & Luisi, 2014; Walsh, 2015; Okasha, 2018). A living system represents a "combination of labor" with an overarching vocation, a means-ends teleonomy. Some theorists (e.g., Gilbert et al., 2012) have adopted the term "holobiont" to characterize this frame shift.

Biologist Patrick Bateson (2013) has illustrated this alternative paradigm with an analogy. The recipe for a biscuit/cookie is rather like the genome in living organisms. It represents a set of instructions for how to make an end product. A shopper who buys a biscuit/cookie selects the "phenotype" – the end product, not the recipe. So, if the recipe survives and the number of cookies multiplies over time, it is only because shoppers like the end product and are willing to purchase more of them.

6 Lamarckism in Evolution

As noted earlier, some contemporary theorists have adopted the concept of "agency" to characterize this defining biological characteristic (e.g., Walsh, 2015; Okasha, 2018). Other theorists have adopted Humberto Maturana and Francisco Varela's concept of "autopoiesis" (e.g., Capra & Luisi, 2014). Agency is a term that is utilized in biology to characterize the ability of a living system to act as an autonomous, self-directed agent – to vary its behavior and its environment "purposefully" in relation to external or internal ("physiological") conditions and goals. When a persistent wolf chases an evasive hare, both are exercising agency – not God's will, or a philosophical concept but an evolved capability for meeting their needs and coping with challenges in their environments. Agency in living systems is a product of an evolutionary "trial and success" process, as Dobzhansky put it.

For the record, the importance of the organism as a self-organized and self-directed agent in evolution can be traced back at least to Jean Baptiste de Lamarck, who proposed that changes in an animal's "habits," stimulated by environmental changes, have been a primary source of evolutionary change over time. Lamarck (1984/1809:114) wrote: "It is not the organs . . . of an animal's body that have given rise to its special habits and faculties; but it is, on the contrary, its habits, mode of life and environment that have over the course of time controlled . . . the faculties which it possesses." Darwin was open to Lamarck's idea, calling it the "use and disuse of parts," and mentioned it no less than twelve times in *The Origin of Species*, (1968/1859). Conversely, late in life Lamarck embraced a precursor of Darwin's natural selection idea (see Corning, 2018: 70). Darwin even offered some possible evidence in favor of behavioral changes:

> Can a more striking instance of adaptation be given than that of a woodpecker for climbing trees and for seizing insects in the chinks of the bark? Yet in North America there are woodpeckers which feed largely on fruit, and others with elongated wings chase insects on the wing; and on the plains of La Plata, where not a tree grows, there is a woodpecker . . . which never climbs a tree! (Darwin, 1968/1859: 215)

However, Darwin's view of the relative importance of behavior as a causal influence in evolution was more guarded: "It is difficult to tell, and immaterial for us, whether habits generally change first and structure afterwards; or whether slight modifications of structure lead to changed habits; both probably often change almost simultaneously."

A "Darwinized" version of Lamarck's insight, called "Organic Selection Theory" made a brief appearance at the end of the nineteenth century. The basic idea was that purposeful behavioral changes could alter the selective context for natural selection. But this proposal was soon overwhelmed and supplanted by "mutation theory" and the later work that led to the Modern Synthesis (see Corning, 2014). The idea that behavior is an influence in evolutionary change was tentatively reintroduced by the paleontologist George Gaylord Simpson (1953) under the neologism of the Baldwin Effect. However, he portrayed it as being of only minor significance in evolution.

A more direct challenge to the gene-centered Modern Synthesis came from the embryologist and geneticist Conrad Waddington (1942, 1952, 1957, 1962, 1975), who challenged the mainstream dogma when he produced experimental evidence for a Darwinized version of the Lamarckian theory of the inheritance of acquired characters that he called "genetic assimilation." Waddington showed that certain developmentally influenced behavioral characters, like sensitivity to various environmental stimuli, could be enhanced through differential selection to the point where the traits would appear "spontaneously," even in the absence of the stimuli. Waddington also became a vocal critic of the gene-centered view of evolution. As he pointed out, "it is the animal's behavior which to a considerable extent determines the nature of the environment to which it will submit itself and the character of the selective forces with which it will consent to wrestle. This 'feedback' or circularity in a relation between an animal and its environment is rather generally neglected in present-day evolutionary theorizing" (Waddington, 1975: 170).

A turning point came with the major conferences and edited volume on *Behavior and Evolution* (Roe & Simpson, 1958). In a landmark follow-up essay on the subject, Mayr (1960) concluded:

> It is now quite evident that ... the evolutionary changes that result from adaptive shifts are often initiated by a change in behavior, to be followed secondarily by a change in structure ... Changes of evolutionary significance are rarely, except on the cellular level, the direct results of mutation pressure ... The selection pressure in favor of the structural modification is greatly increased by a shift to a new ecological niche, by the acquisition of a new habit, or by both.

Mayr did not mention Lamarck, but he characterized these Lamarckian behavioral innovations as the "pacemakers" of evolution. (Mayr's assertion in 1960 also seems to contradict the contrary view that he expressed in his 1961 *Science* paper.)

7 Behavior and Evolution

In fact, the "purposeful" behavior of living organisms has had a major influence in shaping natural selection and the trajectory of evolution over time. It could be said – with Dobzhansky – that the behavior of living organisms exhibits an internal or natural teleology. The term highlights the fact that evolved teleonomic processes and systems can exert a significant causal influence on the properties and actions of living systems, both in themselves and in others. (See especially Vane-Wright, 2014.) Some theorists speak of "agency"; others of "autopoiesis" (or self-maintenance); still others of "cybernetic" (feedback-driven) goal-directedness. I characterize the "ultimate" evolutionary consequences of this dynamic as "teleonomic selection" (Corning, 2018).

A well-documented illustration involves the remarkable tool-using behavior of the so-called woodpecker finch. *Cactospiza pallidus* is one of the fourteen species of highly unusual finches, first discovered by Darwin, that have evolved in the Galápagos Islands, probably from a single immigrant species of mainland ancestors. Although *C. pallidus* was not actually observed by Darwin, subsequent researchers have found that the woodpecker finch occupies a niche that is normally occupied on the mainland by conventional woodpeckers. However, as any beginning biology student knows, *C. pallidus* has achieved its unique adaptation in a highly unusual way. Instead of excavating trees with its beak and tongue alone, as the mainland woodpecker does, *C. pallidus* skillfully uses cactus spines or small twigs held lengthwise in its beak to probe beneath the bark. When it succeeds in dislodging an insect larva, it will quickly drop its digging tool, or else deftly tuck it between its claws long enough to devour the prey. Members of this species have also been observed carefully selecting digging "tools" of the right size, shape and strength and carrying them from tree to tree (Lack, 1961/1947; Weiner, 1994).

What is most significant about this distinctive behavior, for our purpose, is the "downward" effect it has had on natural selection and the genome of *C. pallidus*. The mainland woodpecker's feeding strategy is in part dependent on the fact that its ancestors evolved an extremely long, probing tongue. But *C. pallidus* has no such "structural" modification. In other words, the invention of a digging tool enabled the woodpecker finch to circumvent the requirement for an otherwise necessary morphological change. This behavioral "workaround" in effect provided both a facilitator and a selective shield, or mask. (For a more recent example of social behavior as a facilitator of genetic change, see Shell et al., 2021.)

It is also frequently the case that the teleonomic behavioral choices of one species can become the instrument of natural selection in another species. One example among many can be found in the rainforest of the Olympic National Park, in the state of Washington, where there is intense competition among the towering evergreen trees (western hemlock, Sitka spruce, Douglas fir, and western cedar) inside a crowded forest canopy. Hemlocks produce by far the most seeds and are the best adapted to growing in the low sunlight conditions of the park. However, it is the Sitka spruce that dominate, and the reason is that the abundant Roosevelt elk in the park feed heavily on young hemlock trees and do not feed on the Sitka spruce. In other words, the food preferences of the elk are the "proximate cause" of differential survival between the hemlock and spruce trees (Warren, 2010).

Some Classic Examples

Indeed, behavioral innovations by living organisms are ubiquitous in the natural world. Some of them are legendary. Here are just a few examples:

- One of the most frequently cited examples concerns the discovery in the late 1940s that British blue tits had developed the clever habit of prying open the foil caps from the milk bottles that, in those days, were delivered directly to customers' front stoops. Like those bobbing toy birds that perch on the edge of a water glass, the blue tits then proceeded to dunk their heads and drink the cream. It was reported that the practice spread rapidly and eventually crossed the English Channel (Byrne, 1995; also, Gould & Gould, 1995).
- Also legendary is psychologist Wolfgang Köhler's experiments with chimpanzees in the 1920s. In one case, captive chimpanzees were able to solve the problem of how to reach bunches of bananas that were suspended high overhead by stacking wooden boxes on top of one another to create a makeshift ladder. There was also the feat of a chimpanzee named "Sultan," who learned to join two sticks together to reach through the bars of his cage and rake in food items that were otherwise out of reach (Köhler, 1925; see also de Waal, 2016).
- Primatologist Jane Goodall observed many examples of novel behaviors among the chimpanzees she studied at Gombe Stream in Tanzania. One classic incident involved a low-ranking male in her study group (Mike), who discovered that he could terrorize the other males by banging loudly on an empty steel drum, rolling the drum downhill, and otherwise using it for threat displays. Mike exploited the intimidating effects of his new "weapon"

to rise in the hierarchy and become the dominant male – until the novelty eventually wore off (Goodall, 1986: 75–76).

• Also famous are the experiments by the Nobel Prize–winning entomologist Karl von Frisch on learning in honeybees. One way of testing for creative problem-solving behavior, von Frisch reasoned, is to present an animal with a problem that natural selection could not have anticipated and then observe the response. So, von Frisch contrived an experiment in which *Apis mellifera* foragers were confronted with a unique situation where their artificial food sources were systematically moved further and further away from the hive. In what resembled true insight, the bees learned to anticipate the moves and began to wait for the food at the presumptive new locations (Von Frisch, 1967; see also Gould & Gould, 1995).

• Honeybees are also good problem-solvers. Experienced honeybees normally avoid alfalfa, whose flowers possess spring-loaded anthers (the sacks at the top of the pollen-bearing stamens) that deliver a sharp blow to any bee that attempts to enter. But modern, large-scale agricultural practices sometimes leave the honeybee with the choice of alfalfa or starvation. In these situations, the bees have learned to avoid being clubbed by foraging only among alfalfa flowers whose anthers have already been tripped, or else eating a hole in the back of the flower to reach the nectar (Reinhardt, 1952; Pankiw, 1967).

• The case of Imo, the young female in a Japanese macaque colony, is especially compelling, because this inventive monkey devised two novel food-processing techniques that subsequently spread to other members of her troop. Shortly after primatologists began provisioning a free-ranging group on Koshima Island off the coast of Japan with sweet potatoes in the early 1950s, they observed Imo taking soiled potatoes to a nearby stream, and later to the ocean, to wash them off before eating them. Other members of Imo's troop observed this behavior and began to emulate it. Later on, the researchers decided to provision the animals with wheat, which they scattered on the beach. Again, it was Imo that first began taking handfuls of grain mixed with sand into the water, where she could wash them off and use the water as a natural separator. And again, Imo's innovation soon spread to others (especially the juveniles). Potato washing and grain separation soon became an established cultural pattern in Imo's troop, even after Imo herself had passed away (Kawai, 1965).

8 Mind in Evolution

Over the past half-century, the research on learning and innovation by living organisms – from "smart bacteria" to human-tutored apes and playful dolphins – has grown to cataract proportions. (Indeed, there is now so much of it that some excellent earlier work is being overlooked and forgotten.) The examples are almost endless: worms, fruit flies, honeybees, guppies, stickleback fish, ravens, various songbirds, hens, rats, gorillas, chimpanzees, elephants, dolphins, whales, and many others. (In the index to their book on *Animal Traditions*, Eytan Avital & Eva Jablonka, 2000, list well over 200 different species.)

We now know that primitive *E. coli* bacteria, slime molds, *Drosophila* flies, ants, bees, flatworms, laboratory mice, pigeons, guppies, cuttlefish, octopuses, dolphins, gorillas, and chimpanzees, among many other species, can learn novel responses to novel conditions, via "classical" and "operant" conditioning.

Our respect for the "cognitive" abilities of various animals also continues to grow (see Gibson, 1979/2015; Thompson, 2007; de Waal, 2016). Innumerable studies have documented that many species are capable of sophisticated cost-benefit calculations, sometimes involving several variables, including the perceived risks, energetic costs, time expenditures, nutrient quality, resource alternatives, relative abundance, and more. Animals are constantly required to make "decisions" about habitats, foraging, food options, travel routes, nest sites, even mates. Many of these decisions are under tight genetic control, with "pre-programmed" selection criteria. But many more are also, at least in part, the product of experience, trial-and-error learning, observation, and even, perhaps, some insight learning (Corning, 2014, 2018). One classic illustration is ethologist Bernd Heinrich's experiments in which naïve ravens quickly learned to use their beaks and claws to pull up "fishing lines" hung from their roosts, in order to capture the food rewards attached at the ends (Heinrich, 1995). (Heinrich's 1999 book, *The Mind of the Raven*, provides extensive evidence for the mental abilities of these remarkable birds.)

Indeed, even plants make "decisions." In the marine alga *Fucus*, for example, biologists Simon Gilroy and Anthony Trewavas (2001) have found that at least seventeen environmental conditions can be "sensed," and the information that it collects is then either summed or integrated synergistically as appropriate. Gilroy and Trewavas conclude: "What is required of plant-cell signal-transduction studies . . . is to account for 'intelligent' decision-making; computation of the right choice among close alternatives" (see also Trewavas, 2014).

Especially important theoretically are the many forms of social learning through "stimulus enhancement," "contagion effects," "emulation," and even some "teaching." Social learning has been documented in many species of animals, from rats to bats, to lions and elephants, as well as some birds and fishes and, of course, domestic dogs. For instance, red-wing blackbirds, which readily colonize new habitats, are especially prone to acquire new food habits – or food aversions – from watching other birds (Weigl & Hanson, 1980). Pigeons can learn specific food-getting skills from other pigeons (Palameta & LeFebvre,

1985). Domestic cats, when denied the ability to observe conspecifics, will learn certain tasks much more slowly or not at all (John et al., 1968). And, in a controlled laboratory study, naive ground squirrels (*Tamiasciurus Hudsonicus*) that were allowed to observe an experienced squirrel feed on hickory nuts were able to learn the same trick in half the time it took for unenlightened animals (cited in Byrne, 1995: 58).

True "imitation" (including the learning of motor skills) has also been observed in (among others) gorillas (peeling wild celery to get at the pith), rats (pressing a joy stick for food rewards), African grey parrots (vocalizations and gestures), chimpanzees (nut-cracking with an anvil and a stone or wooden hammer), and bottlenose dolphins (many behaviors, including grooming, sleeping postures, even mimicking the divers that scraped the observation windows of their pools, down to the sounds made by the divers' breathing apparatus) (see Corning, 2014).

Cognition in Social Mammals

Not surprisingly, the most potent cognitive skills have been found in social mammals, especially the great apes. They display intentional behavior, planning, social coordination, understanding of cause and effect, anticipation, generalization, even deception. Primatologists Richard Byrne and Andrew Whiten, in their two important edited volumes on the subject, refer to it as "Machiavellian intelligence" (Byrne & Whiten, 1988; Whiten & Byrne, 1997; also, Gibson & Ingold, 1993; de Waal, 2016). Cognitive skills and social learning have provided a powerful means – which humankind has greatly enhanced – for accumulating, dispersing, and perpetuating novel adaptations without waiting for slower-acting genetic changes to occur.

Tool-use is an especially significant and widespread category of adaptive behavior in the natural world – from insects to insectivores and omnivores – and it is utilized for a wide variety of purposes. As Edward O. Wilson (1975) pointed out in his comprehensive survey and synthesis, *Sociobiology*, tools provide a means for quantum jumps in behavioral invention, and in the ability of living organisms to manipulate their environments. Tool-use results in otherwise unattainable behavioral outcomes (synergies) (Wilson 1975: 172; also, Beck, 1980; McGrew, 1992).

Chimpanzees are particularly impressive tool users. They frequently use saplings as whips and clubs; they throw sticks, stones, and clumps of vegetation with a clearly hostile intent (but rather poor aim); they insert small sticks, twigs, and grasses into ant and termite holes to "fish" for booty; they use sticks as pry bars, hammers, olfactory aids (to sniff out the contents of enclosed spaces), and even as toothpicks; they also use stones as anvils and hammers (for breaking open the proverbial tough nuts); and they use leaves for various purposes – as sponges (to obtain and hold drinking water), as umbrellas (large banana leaves are very effective), and for wiping themselves in various ways, including chimpanzee equivalents of toilet paper and "sanitary napkins" (see especially E.O. Wilson, 1975; Beck, 1980; McGrew, 1992; Wrangham et al., 1994; de Waal, 2016). Not only are chimpanzees proficient as tool-users but they can also make tools. They break off small tree branches and strip them to fabricate ant "wands"; they use their bodies for leverage when they break down larger sticks to make hammers; they work leaves into sponges; and they carefully select stones of the right size and shape for the job at hand and will then carry them to their worksites.

Finally, it is important to emphasize the role of "culture" and cultural transmission in evolutionary change. The debate about the role of culture in other species, like chimpanzees, may still be unresolved, but there can be no doubt that behavioral and cultural evolution played an important role in human evolution (see especially Corning, 2003, 2012, 2018; also, Kingdon, 1993; Foley, 1995; Klein, 1999; Klein & Edgar, 2002; Boyd & Richerson, 2005, 2009; Richerson & Boyd, 2005; Boyd et al., 2011; Foley & Gamble, 2011; Henrich, 2016).

Biologist Richard Dawkins, in his legendary popular book, *The Selfish Gene*, famously characterized living systems, like humankind, as "survival machines – robot vehicles that are blindly programmed to preserve the selfish molecules known as genes" (Dawkins, 1989/1976: ix). We now know that this is definitely not the case. Arguably, it is the other way around; the genes have evolved in the service of living organisms, for the most part, and the exceptions prove the rule.

9 The "Synergism Hypothesis" Revisited

A major theoretical issue in mainstream evolutionary biology over the past two decades has concerned the rise of complexity in nature, and a search has been underway for "a Grand Unified Theory" – as biologist Daniel McShea (2015) characterized it – that is consistent with Darwin's great vision. McShea aspired to identify "some single principle or some small set of principles" that could explain the evolutionary trend toward greater complexity." Likewise, biologist Deborah Gordon (2007) noted that "Perhaps there can be a general theory of complex systems, but we don't have one yet." (See also the outtake at my website http://complexsystems.org.)

As it happens, such a theory already exists. It was first proposed in *The Synergism Hypothesis: A Theory of Progressive Evolution* (Corning, 1983), and it involves an economic (or perhaps bioeconomic) theory of complexity. Simply stated, cooperative interactions of various kinds, however they may occur, can produce novel combined effects – *synergies* – with functional advantages that may, in turn, become direct causes of natural selection. The focus of the Synergism Hypothesis is on the favorable selection of synergistic "wholes" and the combination of genes that produces these wholes. The parts (and their genes) that produce these synergies may, in effect, become interdependent units of evolutionary change.

In other words, the Synergism Hypothesis is a theory about the unique combined effects produced by the relationships between things. I refer to it as Holistic Darwinism because it is entirely consistent with natural selection theory, properly understood. It is the functional (economic) benefits associated with various kinds of synergistic effects in any given context that are the underlying causes of cooperative relationships – and of complex organization – in the natural world. The synergy produced by the whole provides the proximate functional payoffs that may differentially favor the survival and reproduction of the parts, and their genes. (See also Corning, 2003, 2005, 2012, 2018.)

It should be stressed the synergies can very often be quantified. A legendary example among many others (see Corning, 2018) is the way emperor penguins huddle closely together in large colonies, sometimes numbering in the tens of thousands, to share heat during the bitterly cold Antarctic winter. In so doing, they are able to reduce their individual energy expenditures by 20–50 percent, depending upon where they are in the huddle and the wind direction and speed (Le Maho, 1977).

The biologists John Maynard Smith and Eörs Szathmáry (1995, 1999), in their pathbreaking work on the "major transitions" in evolution, came to the same conclusion independently about the causal role of synergy in evolution – although they graciously acknowledged the priority of my 1983 book in one of their two books on the subject. They applied their version of the Synergism Hypothesis specifically to the problem of explaining the emergence of new levels of biological organization over time (see also Corning & Szathmáry, 2015). Maynard Smith (1982) also proposed the concept of Synergistic Selection as (in effect) a subcategory of natural selection. Synergistic Selection refers to the many contexts in nature where two or more genes/genomes/individuals have a shared fate; their combined effects are functionally interdependent.

Thus, cooperative phenomena of various kinds, which are portrayed as being highly constrained and problematic under the predominately competitive assumptions of the Modern Synthesis, are now seen to play an important causal role in living systems, and in evolution. Biologist Richard Michod (1999) asserts that "cooperation is now seen as the primary creative force behind ever greater levels of complexity and organization in all of biology." And Martin Nowak (2011) calls cooperation "the master architect of evolution." However, it is not cooperation per se that has been the "creative force" or the "architect." Rather, it is the unique combined effects (the synergies) produced by cooperation. Beneficial synergies of various kinds have been a prodigious source of evolutionary novelties and the underlying cause of cooperation and increased complexity in evolution over time (Corning, 1983, 2005, 2012, 2018).

Although it may seem like backward logic, the thesis is that functional synergy is the cause of cooperation and complexity in living systems, not the other way around. To repeat, the Synergism Hypothesis is basically an economic theory of emergent complexity, and it applies equally to biological and cultural evolution – most notably in humankind. Indeed, it now appears that social cooperation has been a key to our evolution as a species, and that social synergy is the reason why we cooperate. In a very real sense, we invented ourselves.

10 Synergy and the Bioeconomics of Evolution

Much of the work in complexity science in recent years has been focused on the physical, structural, functional, and dynamical aspects of complex phenomena. However, complex living organisms are distinctive in that they are also subject to basic economic criteria, and to economic constraints. Biological complexity is not simply an historical artifact, much less the product of some exogenous physical trend, force, or "law." Over the years, many candidate laws have been proposed that have claimed to explain complexity in evolution, going back to Jean Baptiste de Lamarck's "power of life" and Herbert Spencer's "universal law of evolution" during the nineteenth century. In the latter part of the twentieth century, the development of new mathematical tools and rise of complexity theory in various disciplines inspired a plethora of new law-like or mechanistic explanations. (See, for example, Kauffman, 1996.) This theme has continued into the new century, as documented in detail in Corning (2018).

The problem with all such deterministic theories is that they explain away the very thing that needs to be explained – namely, the contingent nature of living systems and their fundamentally functional, adaptive properties. As the biologist Theodosius Dobzhansky long ago (1977) pointed out: "No theory of evolution which leaves the phenomenon of adaptation an unexplained mystery can be satisfactory." The purveyors of these theories often seem oblivious to the inescapable challenges associated with Darwin's "struggle for existence" in the natural world, and they discount the economics – the costs and benefits of complexity. Nor can they explain the fact that some 99 percent of all the species that have ever evolved are now extinct. Life is a phenomenon that is at all times subject to the requirement that the bioeconomic benefits (direct or indirect) of any character or trait – including complexity – must outweigh the costs. It is subject to functional criteria and the calculus of economic costs and benefits in any given environmental context.

The basic question, therefore, is what are the advantages of biological complexity? However, there is also a prior question: What is "complexity"? One must start by defining what the term "complexity" means in relation to living systems before examining how – and why – biological complexity has evolved over time.

How to Define Complexity

The issue of how to define biological complexity has been much debated over the years, and it is evident that there is no one correct way to measure it; it can be defined in different ways for different purposes. However, two alternative methodologies are relevant (at least in theory) as ways of characterizing the broad evolutionary trend toward multi-leveled complex systems over the past 3.8 billion years or so, beginning with the origins of life and culminating (temporally at least) in humankind.

One method is structural. A synthetic complexity scale can be constructed from the number of levels of organization (inclusive of social organization), the number of distinct "parts," the number of different kinds of parts, and the number of interconnections among the parts. The other method is functional. A complexity scale can be derived from the number of functionally discrete "tasks" in the division/combination of labor at all levels of organization, coupled with the quantity of "control information" that is generated and utilized by the system. Control information is defined as "the capacity to control the capacity to do work" in a cybernetic process; it is equivalent to the amount of thermodynamic work that a system can perform. Both of these methodologies are relevant here.

There are also various ways of measuring the economic costs and benefits of biological complexity. The "ultimate" measure is, of course, reproductive success. Although the level of personal investment can vary widely in the natural world, an organism must sustain a minimal economic "profit" in order to be able to reproduce itself, and the more offspring it produces, the more profitable it is from an ultimate evolutionary perspective.

However, there are also a many other "proximate" ways of measuring the costs and benefits involved in "earning a living" in nature, and a number of familiar economic criteria are likely to have been important from a very early stage in the history of life on Earth – capital costs, amortization, operating costs, and, most especially, strict economic profitability. The returns had to outweigh the costs. There is, of course, a large research literature and various journals in behavioral ecology and bioeconomics that are focused on just such proximate issues.

Consider the fundamental need for energy capture. Dating back to physicist Erwin Schrödinger's book W*hat Is Life?* in 1944, it has long been appreciated that thermodynamics is of central importance in understanding the nature of life and the challenges of living. Living systems must do work and are subject to thermodynamic entropy and the Second Law. This imposes significant functional requirements. However, there is also a deep tradition in biophysics that assumes away the economic challenges involved in creating "negative entropy" (Schrödinger's neologism). Indeed, there was a school of theorists who have advanced the proposition that energy is somehow a free good and that available energy itself "drives" the process of creating order and organization in the living world (see Corning & Kline, 1998).

A famous experiment in physics, Maxwell's Demon, unwittingly demonstrated why this assumption is incorrect. In a nutshell, there is no way the Demon could create thermodynamic order "without the expenditure of work" (to use Maxwell's own, ill-considered claim for the Demon). Living systems must adhere to the first and only law (so far) of "thermoeconomics," namely, that the energetic benefits (the energy made available to the system to do work) must outweigh the costs required for capturing and utilizing it. From the very origins of life, energy capture and metabolism have played a key role. As biological complexity has increased over time, the work required to obtain and use energy to sustain the system has increased correspondingly. Indeed, improvements in bioenergetic technologies represent a major theme in evolutionary history and, in every case, involved synergistic phenomena.

"Synergistic Selection"

As noted earlier, biologist John Maynard Smith also proposed the concept of Synergistic Selection in a 1982 paper as (in effect) a subcategory of natural selection. Synergistic Selection refers to the many contexts in nature where two or more genes/genomes/parts/individuals have a shared fate; they are functionally interdependent. Maynard Smith illustrated with a formal mathematical model that included a term for "non-additive" benefits (when 2+2 = 5). The idea is also distilled in the catchphrase "the whole is greater than the sum of its parts," which traces back to the *Metaphysics* of Aristotle (ca. 350 B.C., Book H, 1045: 8–10).

However, Synergistic Selection is an evolutionary dynamic with much wider scope even than Maynard Smith envisioned. It includes, among other things, many additive phenomena with combined threshold effects and, more important, many "qualitative novelties" that cannot even be expressed in quantitative terms. There are, in fact, many different kinds of synergy. Synergistic Selection focuses our attention on the causal dynamics and selective outcomes when synergistic effects of various kinds arise in the natural world. The claim is that synergy and Synergistic Selection have driven the evolution of cooperation and complexity in living systems over time, including especially the major transitions in evolution.

One example (among many cited in my 2018 book) is the evolution of eukaryotes. Increased size and complexity can have many functional advantages in the natural world, and eukaryotic cells, inclusive of their complex internal architecture, are on average some 10,000–15,000 times larger than the typical prokaryote. However, this huge size difference requires many orders of magnitude more energy, and the key to solving this functional imperative was a symbiotic (synergistic) union between an ancestral prokaryote and an ancestor of the specialized, energy-producing mitochondria in modern eukaryotic cells. Not only was this potent new combination of labor mutually beneficial for each of the two partners, but it created a pathway for expanding and multiplying those benefits many times over. Some specialized cells in complex organisms like humans may contain hundreds, or even thousands, of mitochondria. Liver cells, for instance, have some 2,500 mitochondria, and muscle cells may have several times that number. To repeat, it could be called a "synergy of scale."

Many things can influence the likelihood of cooperation and synergy in the natural world – the ecological context, specific opportunities, competitive pressures, the risks (and costs) of cheating or parasitism, effective policing, genetic relatedness, biological "pre-adaptations," and especially the distribution of bioeconomic costs and benefits. However, an essential requisite for cooperation (and complexity) is functional synergy. Just as natural selection is agnostic about the sources of the functional variations that can influence differential survival and reproduction, so the Synergism Hypothesis is agnostic about how synergistic effects can arise in nature. They could be self-organized; they could be a product of some chance variation; they could arise from a happenstance symbiotic relationship; or they could be the result of a purpose-driven behavioral innovation by some living organism.

It should also be stressed that there are many different kinds of synergy in the natural world, including (as noted earlier) synergies of scale (when larger numbers provide an otherwise unattainable collective advantage), threshold effects, functional complementarities, augmentation or facilitation (as with catalysts), joint environmental conditioning, risk- and cost-sharing, information-sharing, collective intelligence, animal-tool "symbiosis" and, of course, the many examples of a division of labor (or more accurately, a "combination of labor"). Indeed, many different synergies may be bundled together (a synergy of synergies) in a complex socially organized "superorganism" like leaf cutter ants, or *Homo sapiens.*

Size in Evolution

It should also be noted that size has played a critically important role in evolution, and that there is a close linkage between size and biological complexity, as discussed in depth by biologist John Tyler Bonner in his book *Why Size Matters* (2006). However, size is not an end in itself. It arises because it confers various functional advantages – various synergies of scale. These may include such things as improved mobility, more effective food acquisition, efficiencies in energy consumption, more efficient and effective reproduction, and, not least, protection from predators.

Consider the example of volvocines, a primitive order of aquatic green algae that form into tight-knit colonies resembling integrated organisms. One of the smallest of these colonies (*Gonium*) has only a handful of cells arranged in a disk, while the *Volvox* that give the volvocine line its name may have some 50,000–60,000 cells arranged in the shape of a hollow sphere that is visible to the naked eye. Each *Volvox* cell is independent, yet the colony-members collaborate closely. For instance, the entire colony is propelled by a thick outer coat of flagella that coordinate their exertions to keep the sphere moving and slowly spinning in the water – in other words, a synergy of scale.

Some of the synergies in the *Volvox* were documented in a study many years ago by Graham Bell (1985), and in more recent studies by Richard Michod (1999). The largest of the *Volvox* colonies have a division of labor between a multicellular body and segregated reproductive cells. Bell's analyses suggested some of the benefits. A division of labor and specialization facilitates growth, resulting in a much larger overall size. It also results in more efficient reproductive machinery (namely, a larger number of smaller germ cells). The large hollow enclosure in *Volvox* also allows a colony to provide a protective envelope for its daughter colonies; the offspring disperse only when the parental colony finally bursts apart.

But there is one other vitally important synergy of scale in *Volvox*. It turns out that their larger overall size results in a much greater survival rate than in the smaller *Gonium*. The volvocines are subject to predation from filter feeders like the ubiquitous copepods, but there is an upper limit to the prey size that their predators can consume. The larger, integrated, multi-cellular *Volvox* colonies are virtually immune from predation by these filter feeders.

Quantifying Synergy

It should also be stressed that synergistic effects can be measured and quantified in various ways. In the biological world, they are predominantly related to survival and reproduction. Thus, hunting or foraging collaboratively – a behavior found in many insects, birds, fish and mammals – may increase the size of the prey that can be pursued, the likelihood of success in capturing prey or the collective probability of finding a "food patch." Collective action against potential predators – herding, communal nesting, synchronized reproduction, alarm calling, coordinated defensive measures, and more – may greatly reduce an individual animal's risk of becoming a meal for some other creature.

Likewise, shared defense of food resources – a practice common among social insects, birds, and social carnivores alike – may provide greater food security for all. Cooperation in nest-building, and in the nurturing and protection of the young, may significantly improve the collective odds of reproductive success. Coordinated movement and migration, including the use of formations to increase aerodynamic or hydrodynamic efficiency, may reduce individual energy expenditures and/or aid in navigation. Forming a coalition against competitors may improve the chances of acquiring a mate, or a nest-site, or access to needed resources (such as a watering-hole, a food patch, or potential prey). In all of these situations, it is the synergies that are responsible for achieving greater efficiencies and enhancing profitability.

Testing for Synergy

There are also various ways of testing for synergy. One method involves experiments, or "thought experiments" in which a major part is removed from the whole. In many cases (not all), a single deletion, subtraction or omission will be sufficient to eliminate the synergy. Take away the heme group from a hemoglobin molecule, or the mitochondria from a eukaryotic cell, or the all-important choanocytes from sponges, or, for that matter, remove a wheel from an automobile. The synergies will vanish.

Another method of testing for synergy derives from the fact that many adaptations, including those that are synergistic, are contingent and context specific, and that virtually all adaptations incur costs as well as benefits. Again, the benefits of any trait must, on balance, outweigh the costs; it must be profitable in terms of its impact on survival and reproduction. Thus, it may not make sense to form a herd, or a shoal, or a communal nest if there are no threatening predators in the neighborhood, especially if proximity encourages the spread of parasites or concentrates the competition for scarce resources. Nor does it make sense for emperor penguins in the Antarctic to huddle together for warmth at high noon during the warm summer months, or for Mexican desert spiders to huddle against the threat of dehydration during the wet rainy season. And hunting as a group may not be advantageous if the prey are small and easily caught by an individual hunter without assistance.

Another way of testing for synergy involves the use of a standard research methodology in the life sciences and behavioral sciences alike – comparative studies. Often a direct comparison will allow for the precise measurement of a synergistic effect. Some of the many documented examples in the research literature include flatworms that can collectively detoxify a silver colloid solution that would otherwise be fatal to any one individual; nest construction efficiencies that can be achieved by social wasps compared to individuals; lower predation rates in larger meerkat groups that have more sentinels; higher pup survival rates in social groups of sea lions compared to isolated mating pairs; the hunting success of cooperating hyenas in contrast with those that fail to cooperate; the productivity of choanocytes in sponges compared to their very similar, free-swimming relatives called choanoflagellates, and the difference in nutrient uptake between lichen partnerships and their independent-living cousins.

A "Grand Unified Theory"?

Albert Einstein long ago observed that "a theory is all the more impressive the greater is the simplicity of its premises, the more different are the kinds of things it relates and the more extended its range of applicability" (Corning, 2018). I believe it is both possible and appropriate to reduce a fundamental aspect of the evolutionary process, in nature and human societies alike, to a unifying theoretical framework. Like the concept of natural selection itself, the Synergism Hypothesis involves an "umbrella term" (an open-ended category) that identifies a common causal principle across a very diverse array of phenomena. Synergistic Selection focuses our attention on the causal role that functional synergies have had at every step in the evolution of biological complexity, beginning with the origins of life itself, and especially including the major transitions in evolution; the functional/bioeconomic benefits have always been the key.

The Synergism Hypothesis can also account for the unique trajectory of human evolution, including the transformative influence of cultural evolution. Synergistic behavioral and cultural innovations played a key role at every stage in the process. (There are three chapters that are concerned with this thesis in my 2018 book on *Synergistic Selection: How Cooperation Has Shaped Evolution and the Rise of Humankind*.) It can also help to explain warfare in human societies, as elsewhere in the natural world. Among other things, warfare is a highly synergistic phenomenon.

The Synergism Hypothesis also encompasses the role of both "positive" and "negative" synergies and their selective consequences for a given organism, group, or species. One obvious example is how organized, cooperative predation may be viewed very differently by a group of predators and their prey. Another example is how individuals and business corporations in human societies may benefit in various ways from burning fossil fuels, yet their combined actions also produce global warming (a negative synergy of scale).

It should also be noted that Synergistic Selection is a dynamic that occurs at both the "proximate" (functional) level and the "ultimate" evolutionary levels. Indeed, proximate synergies are in many cases the direct cause of differential survival and reproduction over time. Some predator–prey interactions are, again, a canonical example.

The Synergism Hypothesis also offers an explanation for the ubiquitous role of cybernetic "control" processes in living systems at all levels. (In humankind, we refer to it, variously, as "management," "politics," and "governance.") As Maynard Smith and Szathmáry (1995, 1999) show in detail in their two books on the major transitions in evolution, every new form of organization in the natural world represents a distinct "combination of labor" that requires integration, coordination, and regulation/policing. From eukaryotic protists to Adam Smith's famous pin factory and the emerging global society in humankind, cybernetic governance is a central challenge and a necessary concomitant. (More on this in the final section.)

11 The Evolution of Humankind

As described in detail in my 2018 book *Synergistic Selection: How Cooperation Has Shaped Evolution and the Rise of Humankind*, there were three keys to our remote ancestors' extraordinary success over time: close social cooperation, adaptive innovation, and functional synergy. Our remote bipedal ancestors, the australopithecines, were quite small (about three feet tall) and relatively slow-moving. They could not have survived the harsh physical challenges involved in living on the ground, nor could they have held their own against the many large predators in their East African environment in those days – such as the pack-hunting *Palhyaena* – without foraging together in closely cooperating groups and defending themselves collectively with the tools that they invented for procuring food, and for self-defense (probably digging sticks that doubled as clubs, and perhaps thrown rocks). The result was a game-changing synergy – cooperative outcomes that could not otherwise be achieved.

The other major transitions in the multimillion-year history of our species followed this same basic formula. Cooperation and innovation were the underlying themes, and the synergies that were produced (the bioeconomic benefits) were the reason why our ancestors cooperated, and why they survived. Thus, the emergence of the much larger and bigger-brained *Homo erectus* some two million years ago was a product of a synergistic joint venture, namely, the hunting of big game animals in closely cooperating groups with the aid of an array of potent new tools – finely balanced throwing spears, hand axes, cutting tools, carriers, and (eventually) fire and cooking. Not to mention (quite likely) sequestered home bases, midwifery, and the first baby-sitting cooperatives. It was a collective survival enterprise – a "superorganism," like the leaf cutter ants – and it was sustained by multiple synergies.

The final emergence of modern humankind, perhaps as early as 300,000 years ago, represented a further elaboration of this collective survival strategy; it was novel bioeconomic synergies that enabled the evolution of much larger groups. Each "tribe" was, in effect, a coalition of many biological families that was sustained by a sophisticated array of new technologies – shelters, clothing, food processing, food preservation and food storage techniques, and much else. Especially important were the more efficient new hunting and gathering tools, like spear throwers (which greatly increased their range and accuracy), bows and arrows, nets, traps, and a variety of fishing techniques. Indeed, culture itself (including spoken language) became a powerful engine of cumulative evolutionary change. Our collective survival enterprise – our superorganism – became an autocatalytic engine of growth and innovation (and environmental disruption) as synergy begat more synergy. Some anthropologists have invoked the idea of culture as a "collective brain" (see Corning, 2018).

But most important for our purpose, there is much evidence that these adaptive social behaviors and technological innovations preceded by many generations the anatomical changes that paleoanthropologists have used to define the major stages in our evolution as a species. In other words, over the course of several million years, the human species in effect invented itself through an entrepreneurial process involving gradual cultural innovations that changed our ancestors' relationship to the environment – and to one another. And these changes, in turn, led to the natural selection of supportive anatomical and psychological traits. As biologist Jonathan Kingdon (1993) put it in the title of his insightful book on this theme, we are the *Self-Made Man*.

A Post-Modern Synthesis?

Many theorists these days are calling for a new post-modern, post-neo-Darwinian evolutionary synthesis. Some theorists advocate the adoption of a more elaborate "multilevel selection" model Others speak of an "Extended Evolutionary Synthesis" that would include developmental processes and Lamarckian inheritance mechanisms, among other things. Denis Noble has proposed what he calls an "Integrative Synthesis" that would include the role of physiology in the causal matrix.

Whatever the label, it is clear that a much more inclusive framework is needed, one that captures the full dynamics and interactions among the many different causal influences at work in the natural world. We also need to view the evolutionary process in terms of multi-leveled systems – functional organizations of matter, energy, and information, from genomes to ecosystems. And we must recognize that the level of selection – of differential survival and reproduction – in this hierarchy of system levels is determined in each instance by a synergistic configuration, or network of causes. Indeed, the outcome in any given context may be a kind of vector sum of the causal forces that are at work at several different levels at once.

An "Inclusive Synthesis"

What is needed going forward is a broadly ecumenical paradigm that would provide more of a work plan than a finished product. Perhaps it could be characterized as an "Inclusive Synthesis." It would be an open-ended framework for explaining how, precisely, natural selection "does its work" in any given context (what causal factors influence adaptive changes). It would also represent an ongoing work-in-progress rather than a completed theoretical edifice.

However, the historical process through which multilevel biological systems have evolved over time can be framed as a sequence of major transitions in complexity – from the very origins of life itself to the emerging global society that humankind is now engaged in creating (for better or worse). And, at every level in this hierarchy, we can see the driving influence of synergy and Synergistic Selection. From an evolutionary/biological perspective, complexity has a purpose – or perhaps even many. In any case, biological complexity must ultimately pass the test of being useful for survival and reproduction. Cooperation may have been the vehicle, but synergy was the driver.

Indeed, we must use our growing understanding of the evolutionary process – especially the insights into the role of teleonomy ('agency") and the centrality of cooperative effects (synergies) – to address the at-risk future of life on Earth. We are increasingly in peril.

12 "Unite or Die"

"Unite or die." These historic words were penned by Benjamin Franklin in 1774 when the American colonies were close to a Declaration of Independence from the British Crown. Nowadays these words also apply to the future of all of humankind. We are at an historic choice point for the entire human species and, perhaps, for the very fate of life on Earth. Currently, we are headed toward a dark future, with ever more terrorist attacks, divisive guerrilla wars, and even, possibly, World War Three (including the likely use of nuclear, chemical, and cyber weapons) – not to mention a drastic, irreversible climate change – unless we can soon make a radical course change.

The solution to this growing global challenge is not to rely on some charismatic, self-serving, authoritarian leader. The world tried doing this back in the 1930s, and it did not end well (World War Two). As the ancient Greek political theorist Plato put it more than 2,000 years ago, the problem with this alternative is how do you "control the controllers"? – those self-serving authoritarians.

A better alternative is more effective global governance under the rule of law, with a new social contract that will provide for the basic needs of everyone (a "basic needs guarantee"), along with rewards for merit, and giving back in proportion to what we receive. I call it the "Fair Society" model. We must also make major changes/improvements to the United Nations and create new U.N. agencies with the authority and resources to address our mounting global challenges. All this is spelled out in detail in my 2023 book, *Superorganism: Toward a New Social Contract for Our Endangered Species.* Here I will briefly outline my "prescription."

In the twentieth century, Plato's famous warning against the seductive allure of demagogues/dictators was updated by the British wartime leader, Winston Churchill. Churchill may have had Hitler and Mussolini in mind when he famously quipped: "Democracy is the worst form of government except for all those others that have been tried from time to time."

Plato, in his early writings, envisioned a "philosopher king" – a leader who would combine the absolute power to govern with the dispassionate wisdom of a trained philosopher. This is what he proposed in his seminal political tract, the *Republic* (ca. 375 B.C.). Often overlooked, however, is Plato's subtitle: "Concerning Justice." His ultimate objective was to achieve a just society.

Later on in his life, Plato came to realize that his philosopher-king concept was unrealistic, and, in his last book, *The Laws*, he proposed a "second-best" alternative in which all interests should be represented, and everyone would be subject to the rule of law. The Founding Fathers of the American republic were students of the Greek philosophers and embodied Plato's mature ideas in our Constitution, which has lasted for almost 250 years so far.

American democracy is far from perfect. The electoral college provision is a big compromise/constraint, as is the composition of the U.S. Senate. There is also the deference paid in the Constitution to the institution of slavery, which culminated in our Civil War in the 1860s. And, of course, there is the persisting influence of racial and sexual discrimination, down to the present day. Not to mention the deep economic inequities and gerrymandering – the partisan distortion of election districts. Today, in addition, there are deeply divisive policy differences among us and a resurgence of anti-democratic, authoritarian leaders. However, Churchill got it right. Even the authoritarians these days must use lies and sham elections to legitimize themselves. And they have a very poor record of good governance in the public interest. Is this really what we want? I believe we can do better.

The basic challenge that we all face, and the basic purpose of any organized society, are biological survival and reproduction. We are all participants in a "collective survival enterprise." Each of us has no less than fourteen "basic needs" – absolute requisites for our survival and reproduction over time. These needs are discussed in detail in my 2011 book: *The Fair Society: The Science of Human Nature and the Pursuit of Social Justice.* They include a number of obvious categories like food, water, waste elimination, and physical safety, as well as some categories that are less obvious but equally important, like adequate sleep, thermoregulation, and healthy respiration.

A "Basic Needs Guarantee"

Going forward, our global social contract must include a "basic needs guarantee" for everyone. The case for this prescription is grounded in four propositions: (1) Our basic needs are increasingly well understood and documented; (2) although our individual needs vary somewhat, they are shared by all of us; (3) we are dependent on many others for the satisfaction of these needs; (4) and severe harm may result if they are not satisfied. (There is also much evidence that this prescription has wide public support; see Corning, 2018: 213–216.)

However, there are two other important fairness precepts. Our basic needs must take priority, but it is also important to recognize the many differences in *merit* among us and to reward (or punish) them as appropriate. The principle of "just deserts" is another way of stating this. In addition, there must be *reciprocity, a* proportionate commitment from everyone to support the "collective survival enterprise." We must all contribute a "fair share" to balance the scale of benefits and costs.

Karl Marx popularized this idea with his slogan, "from each according to his ability, to each according to his needs." However, the Communist firebrand Vladimir Lenin tried to impose this system by force in Russia during the twentieth century, and it did not end well.

"The Fair Society" Model

I believe my updated/improved recipe (I call it "The Fair Society" model – *equality, equity and reciprocity*), coupled with global governance and the rule of law, is the model that is needed for our emerging global "superorganism." Democratic global governance under the "rule of law" is an essential framework for coping with our coming survival crisis, but there is one more thing – the values and outcomes in our global economy.

Our ecological crisis has many contributing causes, but the root of the matter is modern capitalism – at once an ideology, an economic system, a bundle of technologies, and an elaborate superstructure of supportive institutions, laws, and practices that have evolved over hundreds of years. Capitalism has the cardinal virtue of rewarding innovation, initiative, and personal achievement, but it is grounded in a flawed set of assumptions about the nature and purpose of human societies and our implicit social contract; in other words, its core values are skewed.

In the idealized capitalist model, an organized society is essentially a "marketplace" where goods and services are exchanged in arms-length transactions among autonomous "purveyors" who are independently pursuing their own self-interests. This model is in turn supported by the assumption that our motivations can be reduced to the efficient pursuit of our personal "tastes and preferences." We are all rational "utility maximizers" – or *Homo economicus* in the time-honored term. This is all for the best, or so it is claimed, because it will, on balance, produce the "greatest good for the greatest number" (the mantra of Utilitarianism). A corollary of this assumption is that there should be an unrestrained right to private property and the accumulation of wealth, because (in theory) this will generate the capital required to achieve further economic growth. More growth, in turn, will lead to still more wealth.

The foundational expression of this model, quoted in virtually every introductory Economics 101 textbook, is Adam Smith's invisible hand metaphor. As Smith expressed it in *The Wealth of Nations* (1964/1776), man is . . . led by an invisible hand to promote an end which was no part of his intention. Nor is it always the worse for the society that it was not part of it. By pursuing his own interest, he frequently promotes that of the society more effectually than when he really intends to promote it . . . . In spite of their natural selfishness and rapacity . . . [men] are led by an invisible hand to . . . advance the interest of the society . . .

The classical economists who followed in Adam Smith's footsteps embellished his core vision in various ways. One of the most important of these early theorists, Léon Walras, claimed that the market forces of supply and demand, if left alone, would work to ensure the efficient use of resources, full employment, and a "general equilibrium." In short, competitive free markets can be depended upon to be self-organizing and self-correcting, and the profits that flow to the property owners – the capitalists – will generate the wherewithal to achieve further growth and, ultimately, the general welfare. The modern Nobel economist Robert M. Solow (1957) summed up what has been called (sometimes derisively) utopian capitalism as a compound of equilibrium, greed, and rationality.

An Odd Utopia

The well-known senior economist Samuel Bowles, in his book-length critique and re-visioning of economic theory with the unassuming title *Microeconomics* (2004), points out that capitalist doctrine offers "an odd utopia." Its strongest claims are generally false; it is unable to make reliable predictions; it removes from its models many of the factors that shape real-world economies; it ignores the pervasive and inescapable influence of wealth and power in shaping how real economies work; and, not least, it's profoundly unfair. It systematically favors capital over labor, with results that are evident in our skewed economic statistics and widespread poverty. Senior economist John Gowdy (1998: xvi–xvii) candidly acknowledges that "Economic theory not only describes how resources are allocated, it also provides a justification for wealth, poverty, and exploitation."

It happens that two more socially responsible alternative models have emerged in recent years. One has the suggestive title "stakeholder capitalism." It calls for institutional arrangements that will equitably advance the interests of all the stakeholders in a society. In other words, merit is a major criterion.

The other alternative, proposed by the Nobel Prize–winning economist Joseph Stiglitz (2024a, 2024b), is what he calls "Progressive Capitalism." He argues that the time has come to abandon what has also been called "Neoliberalism," after such economists Milton Friedman and Friedrich Hayek, in favor of a model that better serves most citizens, including a social safety net – what FDR called freedom from want and freedom from fear. Progressive capitalism, which already exists in some countries, like Norway and Denmark, will better serve the greater good, Stiglitz argues.

So, what are the implications? The well-known comedian Mort Sahl's ironic observation many years ago, that "The Future Lies Ahead," underscores the fact that, as ecologist Kennth Watt put it, "the future is not what it used to be." Indeed, the future starts now, and our species is in serious peril. We must urgently change our basic survival strategy as a species. The time has come for us to have global governance. Because we are now facing massive and prolonged environmental challenges that most countries cannot cope with alone (especially if they start preparing for them only after the disaster has occurred), we must act collectively to build a sustainable global superorganism – or else. Ideally, we should mobilize the needed resources, management systems, organizational capabilities, and trained workers before these crises occur, and we must have an "all-hands-man-your-battle-stations" response when they do.

The idea of "world government" is, of course, hardly new. It is an enduring dream that can be traced back at least to Bronze Age Egypt and the ancient Chinese Emperors. In the modern era, it has been espoused by a great many prominent people. Both the League of Nations and the United Nations, despite their limitations, were incremental steps in this direction. However, in recent decades the traditional idea of a top-down world government has largely been replaced by the more complex, polycentric, democratic vision of "global governance" – a global system of limited self-governing regimes and cooperative action with respect to specific transnational problems and domains, rather than an overarching, unified, all-powerful political authority.

A significant degree of global governance of this nature has already evolved piecemeal over time in various specialized areas – international law, the law of the sea, international aviation, world trade, and more. But there is now an urgent new imperative. As a recent review concluded: Among the different fields of global governance, environmental management is the most wanting in urgent answers to the crisis in the form of collective action by the whole human community.

I believe we need both expanded global initiatives with respect to climate change and other urgent environmental and health problems, and an enhanced role for world governance.

The Global Governance Initiative

Here is my take on what this regime might look like. What I am calling a Global Governance Initiative is grounded in the belief that there must be a major change in the dynamics of global politics and in the relationships between nations. A significant course change will be needed to meet our growing crisis. Our global system of deeply competitive nation states must shift gears and become much more cooperative in order to deal with this overarching challenge. The competition, conflicts of interest, and sometimes bitter animosities that now exist within and between various countries must be subordinated to a collective mission with shared benefits and costs. New financial resources and new organizational capabilities will also be required to stand up to these hurricane-force headwinds. Only if we have an all-out cooperative effort will we be able to cope with the furies that we are facing, I believe.

Our greatest threat may be each other, and a regression into tribalism and violent conflict. Collective violence (warfare) has been one of the major themes in human history, going as far back as the evidence allows us to go. We are now facing the very real prospect of an era of terrorism and "climate wars." Or worse. Equally important, the challenges we face going forward will very often transcend national borders – from mega-droughts to lethal disease pandemics and the growing hordes of climate refugees. These crises will overwhelm the ability of many countries to deal with them unaided. A concerted international effort will be necessary.

The basic idea is to create an overlay of new global-level services and support functions (along with new financial resources) linked to a set of negotiated social contracts with each country, rather than trying to supplant them or deny their sovereign autonomy and impose solutions. In other words, the overall strategy would be to expand the scope and capabilities of existing international institutions, along with some added political constraints (and reforms, in some cases), in return for an array of positive benefits. Call it the incremental reform model, or the big carrot, small stick strategy.

How Do We Get from Here to There?

However, there is an obvious prior question. How do we get from here to there? What we are talking about is a major shift in global politics and governance. There must be a change of "hearts and minds" at all levels within and between the world's deeply divided nations, including especially the leaders and influential citizens in our most powerful countries. They must come to see that it is in their own self-interest, as well as an urgent moral imperative, to lead the way forward to a new global social contract and a collective effort to deal with the challenges we face.

In his important book, *Upheaval*, Jared Diamond (2019) provides several case studies of national crises where a major course change was achieved, and these can provide us with instructive models for the global crisis we face today (see also Diamond, 2005). Among other things, Diamond says, there must be a broad public consensus that a crisis exists and that something must be done about it. There must be a general readiness to make major changes. There must be political initiative and a willingness to take responsibility for responding to the threat. There must be a clearly defined goal and a practicable solution. And there must be competent and skilled leadership to inspire and implement the necessary changes. I would add to this list that there must also be sufficient financial and other resources – the necessary "means."

Historians and social scientists have long debated the question of which plays a more important role in social change. Is it "bottom up" public pressure from ordinary citizens, or "top down" political leadership? Recent research suggests that the answer is both. Some of the most successful examples of major social changes and crisis responses have involved a synergistic combination of both "bottom up" political movements (with strong public support) and effective "top down" leadership. Each one empowers and informs the other, and neither one would have succeeded alone.

Everyone's favorite example is America's entry into World War Two. For several years after the outbreak of the war in Asia and Europe, America remained a deeply isolationist nation that seemed bent on avoiding involvement in the growing international carnage. This changed literally overnight after the Japanese surprise air attack on our Pacific fleet at Pearl Harbor on December 7, 1941. But there was also competent, trusted leadership in President Franklin D. Roosevelt.

It's Pearl Harbor Day

It's now Pearl Harbor Day for our environmental crisis, but there may not be any psychological shock equivalent to the Pearl Harbor attack to catalyze our resolve. Instead, we may have to rely on the alternative model provided by the likes of the women's suffrage amendment in the early twentieth century and the civil rights legislation in the 1960s, where grassroots political movements inspired by effective leaders gradually won converts and built political support until, finally, the economic and political establishment got the message and acceded to major political reforms.

A similar process of education and consensus building (aided, alas, by the increasing frequency of climate-related natural disasters) may be our best hope for avoiding the metaphorical hangman's noose. To paraphrase Samuel Johnson's famous line, nothing concentrates the mind like the prospect of being hanged in the morning. It's time for us all to look ahead and concentrate our minds on this life-and-death challenge.

There is a spreading mood of gloom in various quarters these days about our environmental crisis. I call it the "doomsday caucus." It includes a significant number of the world's leading scientists, as well as many mainstream environmental experts, professional writers, political activists, and many others who have given up hope that there can be any technological, economic, or political fixes for global warming and our ecological "overshoot" as a species. To these pessimists, the apocalypse is already baked in. Anything we do now is too little, too late.

I believe that such defeatism in the face of our global life-and-death crisis provides a classic example of a self-fulfilling prophecy. There is a great deal more that can be done to mitigate the potential future damage and prevent a full-scale ecological Armageddon. I believe that doing everything we can to deal with the crisis is far better than doing nothing. I much prefer the risk of failure to the certainty of failure.

To sum up then, we are confronting an unprecedented survival crisis, where even our worst-case scenarios may not be realistic enough. Menacing new climate-related disasters seem to be an almost daily occurrence these days. Our survival problem clearly transcends and obliterates national boundaries. We are collectively in peril. Any we-vs-they, or "survival of the fittest" response will likely be hugely costly and self-defeating, and we cannot depend on free market capitalism and "market forces" to solve our problems. (See Stiglitz, 2024a, 2024b; also Daly & Cobb, 1994; Porritt, 2005.)

As we have seen, when the have-nots are desperate and have nothing left to lose, they will do desperate things. And so too will desperate nations. We could all pay a terrible price for inaction.

The key to our success as a species has always been cooperation, adaptive innovation, and synergy, and this must also define our path going forward. In order to respond effectively to the destructive challenges that lie ahead, we must mobilize a significant share of the world's surplus wealth and prepare for the future now, because the future is already well underway. We must also undergird everything we do with the Fair Society principles (*equality, equity,* and *reciprocity*), and we must make a collective commitment to a universal basic needs guarantee. Above all, we must have governance at all levels that is dedicated to the Public Trust, and a global economic system and private sector that serves the common good. Everyone must do his/her part for the collective survival enterprise – the superorganism. But, in return, there must be reciprocal benefits for all the stakeholders and contributors.

The very survival of our global superorganism and its many parts must now become our overriding priority, because we are deeply, inescapably interdependent. To echo Benjamin Franklin again, we must all survive together, or we will go extinct separately. It's time to concentrate our minds on the hangman's noose. Both our past and our future as a species – our ancient heritage and our ultimate fate – are calling on us to respond. It's Pearl Harbor Day. The time for us to choose is now.

The challenge that we face going forward was forcefully stated by one of the most distinguished political commentators of the twentieth century, Walter Lippmann, in a 1969 interview in *The New York Times* just before he died. His words, more than ever, ring true:

> This is not the first time that human affairs have been chaotic and seemed ungovernable. But never before, I think, have the stakes been so high ... What is really pressing upon us is that the need to be governed ... threatens to exceed man's capacity to govern. This furious multiplication of the masses of mankind coincides with the ever more imminent threat that, because we are so ungoverned, we are polluting and destroying the environment in which the human race must live.... The supreme question before mankind – to which I shall not live to know the answer – is how men will be able to make themselves willing and able to save themselves.

Almost a half-century later, Lippmann's "supreme question" remains unanswered. We must act now. Later will be too late.

References

Archibald, J. (2014). *One Plus One Equals One: Symbiosis and the Evolution of Complex Life*. Oxford: Oxford University Press.

Aristotle (1961/ca. 350 B.C.). *The Metaphysics*. Cambridge, MA: Harvard University Press.

Avital, E., & Jablonka, E. (2000). *Animal Traditions: Behavioural Inheritance in Evolution*. Cambridge: Cambridge University Press.

Baluśka, F., Miller, W. B. Jr., & Reber, A. S. (2023a). Cellular Basis of Cognition and Evolution: From Protists and Fungi up to Animals, Plants, and Root-Fungal Networks. In Corning, P. A., Kauffman, S. A., Noble, D. et al., eds. *Evolution "On Purpose": Teleonomy in Living Systems*, pp. 34–58. Cambridge, MA: The MIT Press.

Baluśka, F., Miller, W. B. Jr., & Reber, A. S. (2023b). Cellular and Evolutionary Perspectives on Organismal Cognition: From Unicellular to Multicellular Organisms. *Biological Journal of the Linnean Society* 139(3): 503–513.

Bateson, P. P. G. (2004). The Active Role of Behavior in Evolution. *Biology and Philosophy* 19: 283–298.

Bateson, P. P. G. (2005). The Return of the Whole Organism. *Journal of Bioscience* 30: 31–39.

Bateson, P. P. G. (2013). Evolution, Epigenetics and Cooperation. *Journal of Bioscience* 38(4): 1–10.

Bateson, P. P. G., & Gluckman, P. (2011). *Plasticity, Robustness, Development, and Evolution*. Cambridge: Cambridge University Press.

Beck, B. B. (1980). *Animal Tool Behavior*. New York: Garland Press.

Bell, G. (1985). Origin and Early Evolution of Germ Cells as Illustrated by the Volvocales. In Halverson, H. O., & Monroy, A., eds. *Origin and Evolution of Sex*, pp. 221–256. New York: Alan R. Liss.

Bonner, J. T. (2006). *Why Size Matters: From Bacteria to Blue Whales*. Princeton, NJ: Princeton University Press.

Bowles, S. (2004). *Microeconomics: Behavior, Institutions, and Evolution*. New York: Princeton University Press.

Boyd, R., & Richerson, P. J. (2005). *The Origin and Evolution of Cultures*. Oxford: Oxford University Press.

Boyd, R., & Richerson, P. J. (2009). Culture and the Evolution of Human Cooperation. *Philosophical Transactions of the Royal Society of London Series B, Biological Sciences* 364: 3281–3288.

Boyd, R., Richerson, P. J., & Henrich, J. (2011). The Cultural Niche: Why Social Learning Is Essential for Human Adaptation. *Proceedings of the National Academy of Sciences of the United States of America* 108: 10918–10925.

Boyd, R., Richerson, P. J., & Henrich, J. (2013). Cultural Evolution of Technology: Facts and Theories. In Richerson, P. J., & Christiansen, M., eds. *Cultural Evolution: Society, Technology, Language, and Religion*, pp. 119–142. Cambridge, MA: MIT Press.

Byrne, R. W. (1995). *The Thinking Ape: Evolutionary Origins of Intelligence.* Oxford: Oxford University Press.

Byrne, R. W., & Whiten, A., eds. (1988). *Machiavellian Intelligence: Social Expertise and the Evolution of Intellect in Monkeys, Apes and Humans.* Oxford: Oxford University Press.

Calcott, B. (2013a). Why the Proximate – Ultimate Distinction Is Misleading, and Why It Matters for Understanding the Evolution of Cooperation. In Sterelny, K., Joyce, R., Calcott, B., & Fraser, B., eds. *Cooperation and Its Evolution*, pp. 249–263. Cambridge, MA: MIT Press.

Calcott, B. (2013b). Why How and Why Aren't Enough: More Problems with Mayr's Proximate-Ultimate Distinction. *Biology and Philosophy* 28(5): 767–780.

Campbell, J. H. (1994). Organisms Create Evolution. In Campbell, J. H., & Schopf, J. W., eds. *Creative Evolution?!* pp. 85–102. Boston, MA: Jones & Bartlett.

Capra, F., & Luisi, P. L. (2014). The Systems View of Life: A Unifying Vision. Cambridge: Cambridge University Press.

Corning, P. A. (1983). *The Synergism Hypothesis: A Theory of Progressive Evolution.* New York: McGraw-Hill.

Corning, P. A. (2003). *Nature's Magic: Synergy in Evolution and the Fate of Humankind.* Cambridge: Cambridge University Press.

Corning, P. A. (2005). *Holistic Darwinism: Synergy, Cybernetics and the Bioeconomics of Evolution.* Chicago, IL: The University of Chicago Press.

Corning, P. (2011). *The Fair Society: The Science of Human Nature and the Pursuit of Social Justice.* Chicago, IL: University of Chicago Press.

Corning, P. A. (2012). Rotating the Necker Cube: A Bioeconomic Approach to Cooperation and the Causal Role of Synergy in Evolution. *Journal of Bioeconomics* 15: 171–193. https://doi.org/10.1007/s10818-0129142-4.

Corning, P. A. (2014). Evolution "On Purpose": How Behaviour Has Shaped the Evolutionary Process. *Biological Journal of the Linnean Society* 112: 242–260.

Corning, P. (2018). *Synergistic Selection: How Cooperation Has Shaped Evolution and the Rise of Humankind*. Singapore: World Scientific.

Corning, P. A. (2019). Teleonomy and the Proximate-Ultimate Distinction Revisited. *Biological Journal of the Linnean Society* 127(4): 912–916. https://doi.org/10.1093/biolinnean/blz087.

Corning, P. A. (2020). Beyond the Modern Synthesis: A Framework for a More Inclusive Biological Synthesis. *Progress in Biophysics and Molecular Biology* 153: 5–12. https://doi.org/10.1016/j.pbiomolbio.2020.02.002.

Corning, P. (2023a). *Superorganism: Toward a New Social Contract for Our Endangered Species*. Cambridge: Cambridge University Press.

Corning, P. A. (2023b). Culture-Gene Co-evolution: Darwin's Other Theory Comes into View. *Biological Journal of the Linnean Society* 139(4): 563–569.

Corning, P. A., & Kline, S. J. (1998). Thermodynamics, Information and Life Revisited, Part I: To Be or Entropy. *Systems Research and Behavioral Science* 15: 273–295.

Corning, P. A., & Szathmáry, E. (2015). "Synergistic Selection": A Darwinian Frame for the Evolution of Complexity. *Journal of Theoretical Biology* 371: 45–58.

Corning, P. A., Kauffman, S. A., Noble, D. et al., eds. (2023). *Evolution "on Purpose": Teleonomy in Living Systems*. Cambridge, MA. The MIT Press.

Carrapiço, F. (2010). How Symbiogenic Is Evolution? *Theoretical Bioscience* 129: 135–139.

Craig, N. L. (2002). *Mobile DNA II*. Washington, DC: American Society for Microbiology Press.

Craig, N. L., Chandler, M., Gellert, M., Lambowitz, A., & Rice, P. A., eds. (2015). *Mobile DNA III*. Washington, DC: American Society for Microbiology.

Crick, F. (1970). Central Dogma of Molecular Biology. *Nature* 227 (5258): 561–563.

Crisp, A., Boschetti, C., Perry, M., Tunnacliffe, A., & Micklem, G. (2015). Expression of Multiple Horizontally Acquired Genes is a Hallmark of Both Vertebrate and Invertebrate Genomes. *Genome Biology* 16: 50. https://doi.org/10.1186/s13059-015-0607-3.

Daly, H. E., & Cobb, J. B. Jr. (1994). *For the Common Good* (2nd ed.). Boston, MA: Beacon Press.

Darwin, C. R. (1968/1859). *On the Origin of Species by Means of Natural Selection, or the Preservation of Favoured Races in the Struggle for Life*. Baltimore, MD: Penguin.

Darwin, C. R. (1871). *The Descent of Man and Selection in Relation to Sex* (2nd ed.). London: Charles Murray.

Dawkins, R. (1989/1976). *The Selfish Gene*. New York: Oxford University Press.

de Waal, F. (2016). *Are We Smart Enough to Know How Smart Animals Are?* New York: W.W. Norton.

Diamond, J. M. (2005). *Collapse: How Societies Choose to Fail or Succeed*. New York: Viking.

Diamond, J. M. (2019). *Upheaval: Turning Points for Nations in Crisis*. Boston: Little, Brown.

Dobzhansky, T., Ayala, J., Stebbins, J. L., & Valentine, J. W., eds. (1977). *Evolution*. San Francisco, CA: Freeman.

Edelstein, L. R., Smythies, J. R., Quesenberry, P., & Noble, D. eds. (1999). *Exosomes: A Clinical Compendium*. Amsterdam: Elsevier.

Famintsyn, A. S. (1907a). Concerning the Role of Symbiosis in the Evolution of Organisms. Academy of Science, Serial *8, Physical-Mathematical Division* 20(3): 1–14.

Famintsyn, A. S. (1907b). Concerning the Role of Symbiosis in the Evolution of Organisms. *Transactions of the St. Petersburg Society of Natural Science*, 38(1), *Minutes of Session*, 4: 141–143.

Famintsyn, A. S. (1918). What Is Going on with Lichens? *Nature* (April–May): 266–282.

Foley, R. (1995). *Humans before Humanity: An Evolutionary Perspective*. Oxford: Blackwell.

Foley, R., & Gamble, C. (2011). The Ecology of Social Transitions in Human Evolution. *Philosophical Transactions of the Royal Society of London Series B, Biological Sciences* 364: 3267–3279.

Gánti, T. (1971/2003). *The Principles of Life*. Oxford: Oxford University Press.

Gibson, J. J. (1979/2015). *The Ecological Approach to Visual Perception* (Classic Ed.). New York: Psychology Press.

Gibson, R., & Ingold, T. eds. (1993). *Tools, Language, and Cognition in Human Evolution*. Cambridge: Cambridge University Press.

Gilbert, S. F., Sapp, J., & Tauber, A. I. (2012). A Symbiotic View of Life: We Have Never Been Individuals. *Quarterly Review of Biology* 87(4): 325–341.

Gilroy, S., & Trewavas, A. (2001). Signal Processing and Transduction in Plant Cells: The End and the Beginning. *Nature Reviews (Molecular Cell Biology)* 2: 307–314.

Gladyshev, E. A., & Arkhipova, I. R. (2011). A Widespread Class of Reverse Transcriptase-Related Cellular Genes. *Proceedings of the National Academy of Sciences of the United States of America* 108(51): 20311–20316. https://doi.org/10.1073/pnas.1100266108.

Gontier, N. (2007). Universal Symbiosis: An Alternative to Universal Selectionist Accounts of Evolution. *Symbiosis* 44: 167–181.

Goodall, J. (1986). *The Chimpanzees of Gombe: Patterns of Behavior.* Cambridge, MA: Harvard University Press.

Gordon, D. M. (2007). Control without Hierarchy. *Nature* 446: 143.

Gould, J. L., & Gould, C. G. (1995). *The Honey Bee.* New York: Scientific American Library.

Gowdy, J. M., ed. (1998). *Limited Wants, Unlimited Means: A Reader on Hunter-Gatherer Economics and the Environment.* Washington, DC: Island Press.

Grant, B. R., & Grant, P. R. (1979). Darwin's Finches: Population Variation and Sympatric Speciation. *Proceedings of the National Academy of Sciences of the United States of America* 76: 2359–2363.

Grant, B. R., & Grant, P. R. (1989). Natural Selection in a Population of Darwin's Finches. *American Naturalist* 133: 377–393.

Grant, B. R., & Grant, P. R. (1993). Evolution of Darwin's Finches Caused by a Rare Climatic Event. *Proceedings of the Royal Society of London Series B, Biological Sciences* 251: 111–117.

Grant, P. R., & Grant, B. R. (2002). Adaptive Radiation of Darwin's Finches. *American Scientist* 90: 130–139.

Heinrich, B. (1995). An Experimental Investigation of Insight in Common Ravens (*Corvus corax*). *Auk* 112: 994–1003.

Heinrich, B. (1999). *Mind of the Raven: Investigations and Adventures with Wolf-Birds.* New York: Harper Collins.

Henrich, J. (2016). *The Secret of Our Success: How Culture Is Driving Human Evolution, Domesticating Our Species, and Making us Smarter.* Princeton, NJ: Princeton University Press.

Huneman, P., & Walsh, D. M. (2017). *Challenging the Modern Synthesis: Adaptation, Development, and Inheritance.* New York: Oxford University Press.

Hurley, C., & Montgomery, S. (2009). Peppered Moths and Melanism. www.christs.cam.ac.uk/darwin200/pages/index.php?page_id=g5.

Jablonka, E. (2013). Epigenetic Inheritance and Plasticity: The Responsive Germline. *Progress in Biophysics and Molecular Biology* 111: 99–107. https://doi.org/10.1016/j.pbiomolbio.2012.08.014.

Jablonka, E., & Raz, G. (2009). Transgenerational Epigenetic Inheritance: Prevalence, Mechanisms, and Implications for The Study of Heredity and

46 References

Evolution. *Quarterly Review of Biology* 84(2): 131–176. https://doi.org/10.1086/598822.

Jablonka, E., & Lamb, M. J. (2014). *Evolution in Four Dimensions: Genetic, Epigenetic, Behavioral, and Symbolic Variation in the History of Life* (rev. ed.). Cambridge, MA: The MIT Press.

Jacob, F. (1977). Evolution and Tinkering. *Science* 196 (4295): 1161–1166.

John, E. R., Chesler, P., Bartlett, F., & Victor, I. (1968). Observation Learning in Cats. *Science* 159: 1489–1491.

Kauffman, S. A. (1996). *At Home in the Universe: The Search for the Laws of Self-Organization and Complexity.* Oxford: Oxford University Press.

Kawai, M. (1965). Newly Acquired Pre-Cultural Behavior of a Natural Troop of Japanese Monkeys on Kashima Island. *Primates; Journal of Primatology* 6: 1–30.

Kettlewell, H. B. D. (1955). Selection Experiments on Industrial Melanism in the Lepidoptera. *Heredity* 9: 323–342.

Kettlewell, H. B. D. (1973). *The Evolution of Melanism: The Study of a Recurring Necessity.* Oxford: Oxford University Press.

Kingdon, J. (1993). *Self-Made Man: Human Evolution from Eden to Extinction?* New York: John Wiley.

Klein, R. G. (1999). *The Human Career: Human Biological and Cultural Origins*, 2nd ed. Chicago, IL: University of Chicago Press.

Klein, R. G., & Edgar, B. (2002). *The Dawn of Human Culture.* New York: John Wiley & Sons.

Koestler, A. (1967). *The Ghost in the Machine.* New York: Macmillan.

Köhler, M. (1925). *The Mentality of Apes.* London: Routledge Kegan Paul.

Koonin, E. V. (2009). The Origin at 150: Is a New Evolutionary Synthesis in Sight? *Trends in Genetics* 25(11): 473–475. https://doi.org/10.1016/j.tig.2009.09.007.

Koonin, E. V. (2011). *The Logic of Chance: The Nature and Origin of Biological Evolution.* Upper Saddle River, NJ: FT Press, Science.

Koonin, E. V. (2016). Viruses and Mobile Elements as Drivers of Evolutionary Transitions. *Philosophical Transactions of the Royal Society of London, Series B* 371: 20150442. https://doi.org/10.1098/rstb.2015.0442.

Koonin, E. V., & Martin, W. (2005). On The Origin of Genomes and Cells within Inorganic Compartments. *Trends in Genetics* 21: 647–654.

Kozo-Polyansky, B. M. (1924). A New Principle of Biology. Essay on the Theory of Symbiogenesis [in Russian]. Voronezh.

Kozo-Polyansky, B. M. (1932). Introduction to Darwinism [in Russian]. Voronezh.

Lack, D. L. (1961/1947). *Darwin's Finches.* New York: Harper & Row.

Laland, K. N. (2017). *Darwin's Unfinished Symphony: How Culture Made the Human Mind*. Princeton, NJ: Princeton University Press.

Laland, K. N., Odling-Smee, F. J., & Feldman, M. W. (1999). Evolutionary Consequences of Niche Construction and Their Implications for Ecology. *Proceedings of the National Academy of Sciences of the United States of America* 96: 10242–10247.

Laland, K. N., Odling-Smee, F. J., & Myles, S. (2010). How Culture Shaped the Human Genome: Bringing Genetics and the Human Sciences Together. *Nature Reviews, Genetics* 11: 137–148.

Laland, K. N., Odling-Smee, F. J., Hoppitt, W., & Uller, T. (2013). More on How and Why: Cause and Effect in Biology Revisited. *Biology and Philosophy* 28(5): 719–745.

Laland, K. N., Sterelny, K., Odling-Smee, F. J., Hoppitt, W., & Uller, T. (2011). Cause and Effect in Biology Revisited: Is Mayr's Proximate-Ultimate Dichotomy Still Useful? *Science* 334: 1512–1516.

Lamarck, J.-B. (1984/1809). *Zoological Philosophy: An Exposition with Regard to the Natural History of Animals* (Elliot H., trans.). Chicago, IL: University of Chicago Press.

Lane, N. (2009). *Life Ascending: The Ten Great Inventions of Evolution*. New York: W.W. Norton.

Lane, N. (2015). *The Vital Question: Energy, Evolution and the Origins of Complex Life*. New York: W.W. Norton.

Le Maho, Y. (1977). The Emperor Penguin: A Strategy to Live and Breed in the Cold. *American Scientist* 65: 680–693.

Margulis, L. (1970). *Origin of Eukaryotic Cells*. New Haven, CT: Yale University Press.

Margulis, L. (1981). *Symbiosis in Cell Evolution*. San Francisco, CA: W.H. Freeman.

Margulis, L. (1993). *Symbiosis in Cell Evolution* (2nd ed.). New York: W.H. Freeman.

Margulis, L. (1998). *Symbiotic Planet: A New Look at Evolution*. New York: Basic Books.

Margulis, L., & Fester, R. eds., (1991). *Symbiosis as a Source of Evolutionary Innovation: Speciation and Morphogenesis*. Cambridge, MA: MIT Press.

Margulis, L., & Sagan, D. (1995). *What Is Life?* New York: Simon & Shuster.

Margulis, L., & Sagan, D. (2002). *Acquiring Genomes: A Theory of the Origins of Species*. New York: Basic Books.

Martin, W. F., & Russell, M. J. (2003). On the Origin of Cells: An Hypothesis for the Evolutionary Transition from Abiotic Biochemistry to Chemoautotrophic

Prokaryotes, and from Prokaryotes to Nucleated Cells. *Philosophical Transactions of the Royal Society B* 358: 59–85.

Maturana, H. R., & Varela, F. J. (1980/1973). *Autopoiesis and Cognition: The Realization of Living.* Dordrecht: Reidel.

Maynard Smith, J. (1982). The Evolution of Social Behavior – A Classification of Models. In the King's College Sociobiology Group, eds. *Current Problems in Sociobiology,* pp. 28–44. Cambridge: Cambridge University Press.

Maynard Smith, J., & Szathmáry, E. (1995). *The Major Transitions in Evolution.* Oxford: Freeman Press.

Maynard Smith, J., & Szathmáry, E. (1999). *The Origins of Life: From the Birth of Life to the Origin of Language.* Oxford: Oxford University Press.

Mayr, E. (1960). The Emergence of Evolutionary Novelties. In Tax, S. ed. *Evolution after Darwin* (Vol I), pp. 349–380. Chicago, IL: University of Chicago Press.

Mayr, E. (1961). Cause and Effect in Biology – Kinds of Causes, Predictability, and Teleology are Viewed by a Practicing Biologist. *Science* 134(348): 1501–1506. https://doi.org/10.1126/science.134.3489.1501.

Mayr, E. (1963). *Animal Species and Evolution.* Cambridge, MA: Harvard University Press.

Mayr, E. (1974). Teleological and Teleonomic: A New Analysis. In Cohen, R. S., & Wartofsky, M. W., eds. *Boston Studies in the Philosophy of Science* (Vol. XIV), pp. 91–117. Boston, MA: Reidel.

Mayr, E. (1988). *Towards a New Philosophy of Biology.* Cambridge, MA: Harvard University Press.

McClintock, B., & Moore, J. A., eds. (1987). *The Discovery and Characterization of Transposable Elements: The Collected Papers of Barbara McClintock.* New York: Garland.

McGrew, W. C. (1992). *Chimpanzee Material Culture: Implications for Human Evolution.* Cambridge: Cambridge University Press.

McShea, D. W. (2015). Bernd Rosslenbroich: On the Origin of Autonomy; a New Look at the Major Transitions (book review). *Biology and Philosophy* 30(3): 439–446. https://doi.org/10.1007/s10539-0159474-2.

Mereschkovsky, K. C. (1909). The Theory of Two Plasms as the Foundation of Symbiogenesis, a New Doctrine about the Origins of Organisms (in Russian). *Proceedings of the Imperial Kazan University* [USSR] 12: 1–102.

Mereschkovsky, K. C. (1920). La Plante Considérée Comme un Complexe Symbiotique. *Societé des Sciences Naturelles de l'Quest de la France, Bulletin,* 6: 17–98.

Michod, R. E. (1999). *Darwinian Dynamics, Evolutionary Transitions in Fitness and Individuality.* Princeton, NJ: Princeton University Press.

Miller, W. B. Jr. (2023). *Cognition-Based Evolution: Natural Cellular Engineering and the Intelligent Cell*. Boca Raton, Fl: CRC Press.

Monod, J. (1971). *Chance and Necessity* (Wainhouse A. trans.). New York: Alfred A. Knopf.

Müller, G. B., & Newman, S. A., eds. (2003). *Origination of Organismal Form: Beyond the Gene in Developmental and Evolutionary Biology*. Cambridge, MA: MIT Press.

Noble, D. (2006). *The Music of Life: Biology beyond the Genes*. Oxford: Oxford University Press.

Noble, D. (2011). Neo-Darwinism, the Modern Synthesis and Selfish Genes: Are They of Use in Physiology? *Journal of Physiology* 589(5): 1007–1015. https://doi.org/10.1113/jphysiol.2010.201384.

Noble D. (2012). A Theory of Biological Relativity: No Privileged Level of Causation. *Interface Focus* 2: 55–64.

Noble, D. (2013). Physiology Is Rocking the Foundations of Evolutionary Biology. *Experimental Physiology* 98(8): 1235–1243. https://doi.org/10.1113/expphysiol.2012.071134.

Noble, D. (2015). Evolution beyond Neo-Darwinism: A New Conceptual Framework. *Journal of Experimental Biology* 218(Pt 1): 7–13. https://doi.org/10.1242/jeb.106310.

Noble, D. (2017). *Dance to the Tune of Life: Biological Relativity*. Cambridge: Cambridge University Press.

Noble, D. (2018). Central Dogma or Central Debate? *Physiology* 33: 246–249. https://doi.org/10.1152/physiol.00017.2018.

Nowak, M. A. (2011). *Super Cooperators: Altruism, Evolution and Why We Need Each Other to Succeed* (with Highfield, R.). New York: Free Press.

Odling-Smee, F. J., Laland, K. N., & Feldman, M. W. (1996). Niche Construction. *American Naturalist* 147: 641–648.

Odling-Smee, F. J., Laland, K. N., & Feldman, M. W. (2003). *Niche Construction: The Neglected Process in Evolution*. Princeton, NJ: Princeton University Press.

Okasha, S. (2006). *Evolution and the Levels of Selection*. Oxford: Oxford University Press.

Okasha, S. (2018). *Agents and Goals in Evolution*. Oxford: Oxford University Press.

Palameta, B., & Lefebvre, L. K. (1985). The Social Transmission of a Food-Finding Technique in Pigeons: What Is Learned? *Animal Behaviour* 33: 892–896.

Pan, D., & Zhang, L. (2009). Burst of Young Retrogenes and Independent Retrogene Formation in Mammals. *PloS One* 4(3): e5040. https://doi.org/ 10.1371/journal.pone.0005040. www.ncbi.nlm.nih.gov/pubmed/19325906.

Pankiw, P. (1967). Studies of Honey Bees on Alfalfa Flowers. *Journal of Apicultural Research* 6: 105–112.

Pittendrigh, C. S. (1958). Adaptation, Natural Selection and Behavior. In Roe, A., & Simpson, G. G., eds. *Behavior and Evolution*, pp. 390–416. New Haven, CT: Yale University Press.

Porritt, J. (2005). *Capitalism as if the World Matters*. London: Earthscan.

Powner, M. W., Gerland, B., & Sutherland, J. D. (2009). Synthesis of Activated Pyrimidine Ribonucleotides in Prebiotically Plausible Conditions. *Nature* 459: 239–242.

Pross, A. (2024, July 12). The Chemical Roots of Consciousness. *IAI News*. https://iai.tv/articles/consciousness-drives-evolution-auid-2889.

Reinhardt, J. F. (1952). Responses of Honey Bees to Alfalfa Flowers. *American Naturalist* 86: 257–275.

Richerson, P. J., & Boyd, R. (2005). *Not by Genes Alone: How Culture Transformed Human Evolution*. Chicago, IL: University of Chicago Press.

Roe, A., & Simpson, G. G., eds. (1958). *Behavior and Evolution*. New Haven, CT: Yale University Press.

Rosen, R. (1970). *Dynamical Systems Theory in Biology*. New York: Wiley Interscience.

Rosen, R. (1991). *Life Itself: A Comprehensive Inquiry into the Nature, Origin, and Fabrication of Life*. New York: Columbia University Press.

Russell, M. (2006). First Life. *American Scientist* 94: 32–39.

Sapp, J. (1994). *Evolution by Association: A History of Symbiosis*. New York: Oxford University Press.

Sapp, J. (2009). *The New Foundations of Evolution, on the Tree of Life*. Oxford: Oxford University Press.

Schrödinger, E. (1944). *What Is Life? The Physical Aspect of the Living Cell*. Cambridge: Cambridge University Press.

Shapiro, J. A. (1988). Bacteria as Multicellular Organisms. *Scientific American* 258: 82–89.

Shapiro, J. A. (1991). Genomes as Smart Systems. *Genetica* 84: 3–4.

Shapiro, J. A. (2011). *Evolution: A View From the 21st Century*. Upper Saddle River, NJ: FT Science Press.

Shapiro, J. A. (2013). How Life Changes Itself: The Read-Write (rw) Genome. *Physics of Life Reviews* 10: 287–323. https://doi.org/10.1016/j.plrev.2013 .07.001.

Shell, W. A., Steffen, M. A., Pare, H. K. et al. (2021). Sociality Sculpts Similar Patterns of Molecular Evolution in Two Independently Evolved Lineages of Eusocial Bees. *Communications Biology* 4: 253. https://doi.org/10.1038/s42003-021-01770-6.

Shilthuizen, M. (2018). *Darwin Comes to Town: How the Urban Jungle Drives Evolution.* New York: Picador.

Simpson, G. G. (1953). The Baldwin Effect. *Evolution* 2: 110–117. https://doi.org/10.1111/j.1558-5646.1953.tb00069.

Skinner, B. F. (1981). Selection by Consequences. *Science* 213: 501–504.

Smith, A. (1964/1776). *The Wealth of Nations.* (2 Vols.) London: Dent.

Solow, R. M. (1957). Technical Growth and the Aggregate Production Function. *Review of Economics and Statistics* 39(3): 312–320.

Stiglitz, J. (2024a). The Time Is up for Neoliberals. *The Washington Post*, May 13.

Stiglitz, J. E. (2024b). *The Road to Freedom: Economics and the Good Society.* New York: W.W. Norton.

Traulsen, A., & Nowak, M. A. (2006). Evolution of Cooperation by Multilevel Selection. *Proceedings of the National Academy of Sciences of the United States of America* 103: 10952–10955.

Trewavas, A. (2014). *Plant Behaviour and Intelligence.* Oxford: Oxford University Press.

Vane-Wright, R. I. (1996). Identifying Priorities for the Conservation of Biodiversity: Systematic Biological Criteria within a Socio-political Framework. In Gaston, K. J., ed., *Biodiversity: A Biology of Numbers and Difference*, pp. 309–344. Oxford: Blackwell.

Vane-Wright, R. I. (2009). Planetary Awareness, Worldviews and the Conservation of Biodiversity. In Kellert, S. R. & Speth, J. G., eds., *The Coming Transformation. Values to Sustain Human and Natural Communities*, pp. 353–382. New Haven, CT: Yale School of Forestry & Environmental Studies.

Vane-Wright, R. I. ed. (2014). The Role of Behaviour in Evolution. Special Issue. *Biological Journal of the Linnean Society.*112(2): [ii] + 219–365.

Von Frisch, K. (1967). *The Dance Language and Orientation of Bees* (Chadwick L. trans.). Cambridge, MA: Harvard University Press.

Wächtershäuser, G. (1988). Before Enzymes and Templates: Theory of Surface Metabolism. *Microbiology and Molecular Biology Reviews* 52(4): 452–484.

Waddington, C. H. (1942). Canalization of Development and the Inheritance of an Acquired Character. *Nature* 150: 563–565.

Waddington, C. H. (1952). Selection for the Genetic Basis for an Acquired Character. *Nature* 169: 625–626.

Waddington, C. H. (1957). *The Strategy of the Genes. A Discussion of Some Aspects of Theoretical Biology*. New York: Macmillan.

Waddington, C. H. (1962). *New Patterns in Genetics and Development*. New York: Columbia University Press.

Waddington, C. H. (1975). *The Evolution of an Evolutionist*. Ithaca, NY: Cornell University Press.

Walsh, D. M. (2015). *Organisms, Agency, and Evolution*. Cambridge: Cambridge University Press.

Warren, H. C. (2010). *Olympic: The Story Behind the Scenery*. Wickenburg, AZ: KC Publications.

Weigl, P. D., & Hanson, E. V. (1980). Observational Learning and the Feeding Behavior of the Red Squirrel *Tamiasciurus hudsonicus*: The Ontogeny of Optimization. *Ecology* 61: 213–218.

Weiner, J. (1994). *The Beak of the Finch*. New York: Vintage Books.

Weismann, A. (1892). *Das Keimplasma: Eine Theorie der Vererbung* [The Germ Plasm: A Theory of Inheritance]. Jena, Austria: Fischer.

West-Eberhard, M. J. (2003). *Developmental Plasticity and Evolution*. Oxford: Oxford University Press.

West-Eberhard, M. J. (2005a). Developmental Plasticity and the Origin of Species Differences. *Proceedings of the National Academy of Sciences of the United States of America*. 102 (Suppl. 1), 6543–6549. https://doi.org/10.1073/pnas.0501844102.

West-Eberhard, M. J. (2005b). Phenotypic Accommodation: Adaptive Innovation Due to Phenotypic Plasticity. *Journal of Experimental Zoology* 304B: 610–618.

Whiten, A., & Byrne, R. W. (1997). *Machiavellian Intelligence II: Extensions and Evaluations*. Cambridge: Cambridge University Press.

Wilson, E. O. (1975). *Sociobiology: The New Synthesis*. Cambridge, MA: Harvard University Press.

Wilson, D. S. (1997). Introduction: Multilevel Selection Theory Comes of Age. *American Naturalist* 150 (Suppl.): S1–S4. https://doi.org/10.1086/286046.

Witt, D. (2024). Is Vitalism Making a Comeback? *Evolution News*. May 21.

Wrangham, R. W., McGrew, W. C., de Waal, F. B. M., & Heltne, P. G. eds. (1994). *Chimpanzee Cultures*. Cambridge, MA: Harvard University Press.

About the Author

Peter A. Corning, taught for many years in the interdisciplinary Human Biology Program at Stanford University. (He is now retired.) He holds an interdisciplinary doctorate from New York University and won a post-doctoral fellowship in evolutionary biology and behavioral genetics at the Institute for Behavioral Genetics at the University of Colorado. In the year 2000, he was also the President of the International Society for the Systems Sciences. He is the author of nine books and more than 200 journal articles and edited book chapters.

Cambridge Elements ☰

Applied Evolutionary Science

David F. Bjorklund
Florida Atlantic University

David F. Bjorklund is a Professor of Psychology at Florida Atlantic University in Boca Raton, Florida. He is the Editor-in-Chief of the *Journal of Experimental Child Psychology*, the Vice President of the Evolution Institute, and has written numerous articles and books on evolutionary developmental psychology, with a particular interest in the role of immaturity in evolution and development.

Editorial Board

About the Series

This series presents original, concise, and authoritative reviews of key topics in applied evolutionary science. Highlighting how an evolutionary approach can be applied to real-world social issues, many Elements in this series will include findings from programs that have produced positive educational, social, economic, or behavioral benefits. Cambridge Elements in Applied Evolutionary Science is published in association with the Evolution Institute.

 THE EVOLUTION INSTITUTE

Cambridge Elements ≡

Applied Evolutionary Science

Elements in the Series

Printed in the United States
by Baker & Taylor Publisher Services